THE

BRITISH FLORA;

OR,

GENERA AND SPECIES

OF

BRITISH PLANTS:

ARRANGED AFTER THE

Reformed Sexual System;

AND ILLUSTRATED BY

NUMEROUS TABLES, AND DISSECTIONS.

BY

ROBERT JOHN THORNTON, M.D.

PROFESSOR OF BOTANY AT GUY'S, MEMBER OF THE UNIVERSITY OF
CAMBRIDGE, AND OF THE ROYAL LONDON COLLEGE OF PHYSICIANS,
&c. &c. &c.

___

VOL. V.

═══════

London:

Printed for the Author by J. WHITING, Finsbury Place, as Prizes for the Royal Botanical Lottery

___

1812.

Class XII. *Polyandria.* Order VI. *Polygynia.*

GENUS 419.

FRAGARIA. *Strawberry.*

(From ᴛʀᴀɢʀᴏ, L. *to smell sweet;*—the English from the Saxon word, ꜱᴛʀᴀᴡ, *herb,* and *berry.*)

THE NATURAL CHARACTERS.

I. Cᴀʟʏx. *Perianth* one-leaved, flat, ten-cleft; *alternate segments* outer, narrower.

II. Cᴏʀᴏʟʟᴀ. *Petals* five, roundish, spreading, inserted in the calyx.

III. Sᴛᴀᴍɪɴᴀ. *Filaments* twenty, awl-shaped, shorter than the corol, inserted in the calyx. *Anthers* half-moon-shaped.

IV. Pɪꜱᴛɪʟʟᴜᴍ. *Stigmas* simple. *Styles* simple, inserted in the sides of the germens. *Germens* numerous, very small, collected into a head.

V. Pᴇʀɪᴄᴀʀᴘ, none. A Berry, is the *common Receptacle* of the seeds, round-ovate, pulpy, soft, large, coloured, truncated at the base, deciduous.

VI. Sᴇᴇᴅꜱ, numerous, very small, acuminate, scattered over the surface of the receptacle.

Note.—The common receptacle is generally esteemed a berry.

THE SECONDARY CHARACTERS.

I. Sᴛᴇᴍ, scaped, many-flowered.

II. Lᴇᴀᴠᴇꜱ, radical, petioled, ternate; leaflets sessile, intire.

III. Fʟᴏᴡᴇʀꜱ, radical, peduncled, white.

IV. Hᴀʙɪᴛᴀᴛɪᴏɴ, woods, barren pastures.

Of this Genus there are two Species.

Class XII. *Polyandria.* Order VI. *Polygynia.*

GENUS 420.

GEUM. *Geum.*

(From ΓΕΥΩ, G. *to taste*, its roots being supposed to resolve a bad taste from the stomach. Pl. 1. 26. c. 7. The same is called *benoite*, in French (Herba benedicta), from its salutary qualities.)

THE NATURAL CHARACTERS.

I. CALYX. *Perianth* one-leaved, ten-cleft, rather erect; *alternate segments* very small, acute.

II. COROLLA. *Petals* five, rounded; *claws* as long as the calyx, narrow, inserted in the calyx.

III. STAMINA. *Filaments* numerous, awl-shaped, the length of the calyx, in which they are inserted. *Anthers* short, broadish, obtuse.

IV. PISTILLUM. *Stigmas* simple. *Styles* inserted in the sides of the germens, hairy, long. *Germens* numerous, collected into a head,

V. PERICARP, none. *Common Receptacle* of the *seeds* oblong, hirsute, placed upon the reflexed calyx.

VI. SEEDS, numerous, compressed, hispid, awned with a long geniculate *style.*

THE SECONDARY CHARACTERS.

I. STEM, herbaceous, round, ramous.

II. LEAVES, inferior lyrate-pinnate, superior digitate-pinnate; leaflets simple.

III. FLOWERS, peduncled, axillary, terminal, and single, yellow,

IV. HABITATION, woods, moist meadows.

Of this Genus there are two Species.

Class XII. *Polyandria.* Order VI. *Polygynia,*

GENUS 421.

POTENTILLA. *Potentilla.*

(A POTENTIA, from its superior efficacy.)

THE NATURAL CHARACTERS.

I. CALYX. *Perianth* one-leaved, flattish, half-ten-cleft; the *alternate segments* less, reflexed.

II. COROLLA. *Petals* five, roundish, spreading, inserted by the claws in the calyx.

III. STAMINA. *Filaments* twenty, awl-shaped, shorter than the corol, inserted in the calyx. *Anthers* elongated, half-moon-shaped.

IV. PISTILLUM. *Stigmas* obtuse. *Styles* filiform, the length of the stamens, inserted in the side of the germen. *Germens* numerous, very small, collected into a head.

V. PERICARP, none. *Common Receptacle* of the *seeds* roundish, juiceless, very small, permanent, covered by the seeds, included in the calyx.

VI. SEEDS, numerous, acuminate.

Note.—Take away one-fifth part of the number in all the parts of fructification, and you will have *Tormentilla.*

THE SECONDARY CHARACTERS.

I. STEM, herbaceous, round, repent or erect.

II. LEAVES, alternate, petioled, equally or interruptedly pinnate, or digitate; leaflets simple, intire.

III. FLOWERS, peduncled, peduncles axillary, terminal, one or many-flowered.

IV. HABITATION, moist meadows, Alpine rocks, gravelly pastures, Scotch Alps, Welch Alps.

Of this Genus there are eight Species.

Class XII. *Polyandria.* Order VI. *Polygynia.*

GENUS 422.

COMARUM. *Cinquefoil.*

(From κεο, G. *to lie down*, being partly procumbent;—the English from its having five leaflets.)

THE NATURAL CHARACTERS.

I. CALYX. *Perianth* one-leaved, ten-cleft, very large, spreading, coloured, permanent; the *alternate segments* smaller, lower.

II. COROLLA. *Petals* five, oblong, acuminate, three times less than the calyx, in which they are inserted.

III. STAMINA. *Filaments* twenty, awl-shaped, inserted in the calyx, the length of the corol, permanent. *Anthers* half-moon-shaped, deciduous.

IV. PISTILLUM. *Stigmas* simple. *Styles* simple, short, from the side of the germen. *Germens* numerous, roundish, very small, collected into a head.

V. PERICARP, none. *Common Receptacle* of the *seeds* ovate, fleshy, very large, permanent.

VI. SEEDS, numerous, acuminate, covering the receptacle.

THE SECONDARY CHARACTERS.

I. STEM, partly procumbent.
II. LEAVES, pinnated.
III. FLOWERS, single, terminal, large, purple.
IV. HABITATION, spungy bogs.

Of this Genus there is one Species.

END OF VOL IV.

CUI BONO?

THE PROPERTIES OF BRITISH PLANTS.

Class I. *Monandria.*

Order I. *Monogynia.*

SALICORNIA HERBACEA. *Marsh Samphire, jointed Glass-Wort, or Salt-Wort.* This plant is common in our sea-coasts, and burnt, so as to produce an alkali used in making glass. The tender shoots of this plant are used as a pickle and sometimes boiled for the table.

Order III. *Gynandria;*

ARUM MACULATUM. *Wake-Robin, or Cuckow-Pint.* The whole plant is extremely acrimonious to the taste, and inflaming the mouth for a long time afterwards; but the roots when boiled or dried lose all their acrimony, and become perfectly insipid, and being of a farinaceous quality have sometimes been made into bread and starch. They are esteemed good in asthmatic complaints, but are rarely used in the present practice, except as a sternutatory to relieve headachs.

ZOSTERA MARINA. *Grass-Wrack. Linnæus* informs us, that the humble inhabitants of Gothland in Sweden condescend to thatch their houses, stuff their beds, and manure their land with this plant.

Class II. *Diandria.*

Order I. *Monogynia.*

VERONICA OFFICINALIS. *Male Speedwell.* This is used as a small drink in colds.

4

VERONICA RECCABUNGA. *Common Brooklime.* It is esteemed an antiscorbutic; and eaten by some in the spring as a sallet, but is more bitter, and not so agreeable to the palate as *Water-cresses.* The flowers are of a fine blue, and the leaves smooth, thick, and succulent.

PINGUICULA VULGARIS, *Common Butter-wort.* The inhabitants of Lapland, and the North of Sweden, give to milk the consistence of cream, by pouring it warm from the cow upon the leaves of this plant, and then instantly straining it, and laying it aside for two or three days till it acquires a degree of acidity. This milk they are extremely fond of; and when once made, they need not repeat the use of the leaves as above, for a spoonful, or less of it, will turn another quantity of warm milk, and make it like the first, and so on as often as they please to renew their food.

Order II. *Digynia.*

ANTHOXANTHUM ODORATUM. *Vernal Grass.* This is one of the earliest blowing grasses, and gives that most agreeable odour to hay.

Order III. *Gynandria.*

ORCHIS BIFOLIA. *Butterfly Orchis.* The roots of this and most of the other kind is highly nutritious.

———— MASCULA. *Male Orchis.* The spikes of these flowers are the *Long-Purples,* or *dead men's fingers,* which helped to compose poor *Ophelia's* garlands:

There with fantastic garlands did she come,
Of crow-flowers, nettles, daisies, and *long purples,*
(That liberal shepherds give a grosser name,)
But our cold maids do *dead men's fingers* call them.

HAMLET, ACT 4.

The *salep* of the shops is made, for the most part, of the roots of this *Orchis;* for this purpose the largest and plumpest bulbs must be gathered, skinned, and boiled over a gentle fire for half an hour; afterwards they must be strung upon a thread, and hung up in the shade till they are dry. These, reduced to powder, are the *salep,* esteemed as a restorative, and therefore reckoned serviceable also in dysenteries, and phthisicky complaints.

Order IV. *Monœcia.*

LEMNA MINOR. *Less Duck's-meat.* It produces its flowers in the Dog-days, which together with the seeds, afford a nourishment to that wonderful animalcule called the Hydra Polypus. Lin. Ducks are well known to be fond of this plant, and the Phalœna Lemnata of Linnæus, breeds upon it.

Order V. *Diœcia.*

SALIX PENTANDRIA. *Sweet Bay-leaved Willow.* The catkins are very sweet scented. The down of the seeds, mixed with a third part of cotton, has been proved to be a very good substitute for cotton itself. Goldfinches, and some other birds, line their nests with the down of this and other species of the genus. The Swedes in Scania dye a yellow colour with the leaves.

———— AMYGDALINA. *Almond-leaved Willow.* The twigs of this kind are used for making baskets.

———— FRAGILIS. *Crack-willow.* This tree is sometimes planted by the sides of walks. The males grow up speedily, and soon form a shade. Bees are fond of the male flowers of this, and other species.

———— LAPONUM. *Woolly Lapland Willow.* This willow, and the *Betula nana,* are the constant summer fuel of the Laplanders, while they attend their rein-deer dairy on the Alps of the North.

———— CAPREA. *Common Sallow.* The inhabitants of the Highlands and Hebrides frequently use the bark of these to tan their leather. The wood is smooth, soft, white, and flexible. It is often used to make handles for hatchets, prongs, spades, &c. and to furnish shoemakers with cutting-boards, and whetting-boards, to smooth the edges of their knives upon. The caterpillars of numerous Phalæna, and other insects, feed upon the leaves of this and the other species of the genus.

———— VIMINALIS. *The Osier.* The twigs are much used for making baskets, bird-cages, and for hooping wooden bottles, &c.

———— ALBA. *Common White Willow.* This is a good tree to plant in avenues, being very speedy of growth, and affording an agreeable shade, and beautiful silvery appearance. The wood and young branches are pliant, the old ones brittle.

The bark will tan leather, and dye yarn of a cinnamon colour, and is of a quality so very astringent, that in a scruple to a dose, it has been found of great service in intermittent fevers. Haller affirms from his own experience, that a bath made of the decoction of it, proved very beneficial to children troubled with rickets.

The inner bark has afforded a miserable substitute for bread to the necessitous inhabitants of Kamtschatka.

The wood is used to make poles, stakes, hoops for casks, &c. and for fuel.

Cattle will feed on the leaves; and the Arabs distil their celebrated Calaf water from the catkins of the S. *Ægyptiaca Lin.* or any other species that has fragrant catkins. This water they use as a cooling liquor, or as a febrifuge.

In the Summer season the leaves have been observed to distil a clear liquor, which Scopoli affirms to be owing to the liquefaction of the spume which envelops an insect called Cicada spumaria. Scop. Entomolog. 331. & Flor. Carniol. 1212.

Order. VI. *Polygamia, Diœcia.*

FRAXINUS EXCELSIOR. *The Ash Tree.* The wood is much used by the wheel-wright for ploughs, and also for carts, and by the cooper for hoops. Horses and sheep are fond of the leaves. The bark and seeds are reckoned a diuretic.

In warm climates a kind of sweet gum, called manna, distils from this tree, two ounces of which is a gentle cathartic.

It is a hardy tree, that endures well the sea-winds, and may therefore be planted upon the shores where few others will grow.

In many parts of the highlands, at the birth of a child, the nurse or midwife, from what motive I know not, puts one end of a green stick of this tree into the fire, and, while it is burning, receives into a spoon the sap or juice which oozes out at the other end, and administers this as the first spoonful of liquor to the new-born babe.

Class III. *Triandria.*
Order I. *Monogynia.*

VALERIANA OFFICINALIS. *Great Wild Valerian.* The roots powdered, and given in large doses, cure the Epilepsy. Cats are very fond of the smell of it.

VALERIANA LOCUSTA. *Corn-sallet.* The radical leaves are used for this purpose.

IRIS PSEUCEDANUS. *Yellow Water Flower-de-luce.* In Arran, and some other Western isles, the roots are used to dye black; and in Jura they are boiled with copperas to make ink.

Order II. *Digynia.*

ALOPECURUS PRATENSIS. *Meadow Fox-tail-grass.* It is esteemed a good grass for hay.

DACTYLIS GLOMERATUS. *Rough Cock's-foot-grass.* This is a very troublesome creeping grass in a garden, and difficult to be destroyed. The gardeners call this, and several other creeping kinds, *Couch-Grass.* It makes a productive grass, when cultivated.

ELYMUS ARENARIUS. *Sea Lime-grass.* The leaves are channeled, rigid, and pungent: the spike linear, downy, and about eight or nine inches long. The creeping roots of this grass, and the *arundo arenaria,* confine the sea sands from being blown about by the winds, and by that means prevent often very destructive inundations.

MELICA CŒRULEA. *Purple Melic-grass.* This grass is readily distinguished by it's black purple panicle: it has a bulbous root, blue antheræ, and a purple pistil, with two or three flowers in a calyx. The fishermen in the isle of Skie make ropes for their nets of this grass, which they find by experience will bear the water well without rotting.

POA TRIVIALIS. *Common Meadow-grass.*

——— ANGUSTIFOLIA. *Narrow-leaved ditto.*

——— PRATENSIS. *Great ditto.* These three grasses are esteemed amongst our best grasses for hay.

AVENA FATUA. *Bearded Oat-grass.* The beard of this is well known to make a very sensible hygrometer. The seeds are of a hairy kind.

FESTUCA OVINA. *Sheep's Fescue-grass.* It is an excellent grass for sheep pastures.

——— ELATIOR. *Lofty ditto.* It is a grass that makes most exlent fodder for cattle.

——— FLUITANS. This grass is of a succulent nourishing quality, and cattle are very fond of it. It would doubtless be a good kind to sow in wet meadows.

The seeds of this grass are in Poland and Germany brought to the tables of the great, as an agreeable and nourishing food, under the name of *Manna Seeds*.

LOLIUM TEMULENTUM. *Annual Darnel-grass*. The seeds of this will intoxicate man, birds, and beasts; and taken in any considerable quantity will bring on convulsions and death. Haller. Helvet, 205, 206.

CYNOSURUS CRISTATUS. *Crested Dog's-tail-grass*. This is esteemed an excellent grass to feed sheep and deer.

Order IV. *Monœcia*.

BRYONIA ALBA. *White Bryony*. The roots are very large, white, and branched, and by the help of moulds, have been formed into a human shape, and exhibited to the ignorant for mandrakes.

TYPHA LATIFOLIA. *Great Cat's-tail, or Reed-mace*. Cattle will sometimes eat the leaves, but Schreber thinks them noxious: the roots have sometimes been eaten in salads, and the down of the *Amentum* used to stuff mattresses and cushions: and Linnæus informs us, that the leaves are used by the coopers in Sweden to bind the hoops of their casks. In England the coopers use the stalks of the *Scirpus lacustris*, or *Bull-rush*, to fasten the joints of the timber in the heads of their casks. One stalk opened longitudinally, and laid between each juncture, answers the intention, as it prevents the oozing of the liquor through it.

CAREX SYLVATICA. *Wood Carex*. Linnæus informs us, that the Laplanders comb and dress this species of *Carex* as we do flax, and in the winter season stuff their shoes and gloves with it, as a defence against the extreme rigour of the climate. They apply some other species to the same purpose, but this seems to have the preference in common use.

———— ACUTA. *Great sharp Vernal ditto*. In Italy the leaves of this plant are used by the glass-makers to bind their wine-flasks, by the chair-makers to bottom chairs, and by the coopers to place between the junctures of the timber in the heads of their casks, in the same manner as the leaves of the *Typha* are used in the same country, and the stalks of the *Scirpus lacustris* in England.

EMPETRUM NIGRUM. *Crake-berries.* The Highlanders frequently eat the berries, but they are no very desirable fruit. If taken too copiously they are reported sometimes to bring on a slight head-ach. Boiled in alum-water they will dye yarn of a black fuscous colour.

Order VI. *Polygamia.*

HOLCUS LANATUS. *Meadow Soft-grass.* This grass is esteemed a good fodder for cattle.

In the isle of Skie it is sometimes used to make ropes for the fishing-boats, but is not so great for that purpose as the *Melica cærulea.* Lin.

Class IV. *Tetrandria.*

FOUR STAMINA.

Order I. *Monogynia.*

DIPSACUS FULLONUM. *Wild Teasel.* Used for carding of cloth.

RUBIA PEREGRINA. *Wild Madder.* It forms a red dye.

GALIUM VERUM. *Yellow Ladies' Bedstraw.* In Arran, and some of the Wes'ern islands, the inhabitants make a strong decoction of this herb, and use it as a rennet to curdle milk ; and in Jura, Uist, and Lewis, &c. I was informed they used the to dye a very fine red, not inferior to that from *madder* itself, but the roots are small.

———————— APPARINE. *Cleavers or Goose-grass.* Linnæus tells us that the Swedes filtrate their milk through a quantity of the stalks of this herb: an observation that may possibly be of use to such who are destitute of proper strainers for that purpose.

CORNUS SUECICA. *Dwarf Honeysuckle, and Plant of Gluttony.* This elegant plant is about six inches high. The berries have a sweet waterish taste, and are supposed by the Highlanders to create a great appetite, whence the Erse name of the plant. Mr. Stuart.

Order IV. *Monæcia.*

BETULA ALBA. *Birch Tree.* Various are the œconomical uses of

·this tree. The Highlanders use the bark to tan their leather, and to make ropes. The outer rind, which they call *Meilleag*, they sometimes burn instead of candles. With the fragments of it, dexterously braided or interwoven, the Laplanders make themselves shoes and baskets. Large thick expanded pieces, with a hole in the middle to fit the neck, they use instead of a *surtout* to keep off the rain. The Americans make entire canoes of it; and the Russians, Poles, and Swedes, in lieu of tiles, cover their houses with it.

The inner bark, before the invention of paper, was used by the ancients to write upon. The wood was formerly used by the Highlanders to make their arrows, but is now converted to better purposes, being used by the wheelwright for ploughs, carts, and most of the rustic implements; by the turner for trenchers, bowls, ladles, &c. the knotty excrescencies affords a beautiful veined wood; and by the cooper for hoops. To which may be added, that it affords excellent fuel, and makes the best of charcoal, and the soot is a good lamp-black for making of printer's ink.

The celebrated *Moxa*, or touchwood, of the Laplanders, used by them as a cautery in most acute disorders, is made of the yellow fungous excrescencies of the woody part of this tree, which sometimes swell out between the fissures and crevices of it, and resemble in substance the agaric.

The leaves are a fodder for sheep and goats, and yield a yellow dye.

The catkins are the favourite food of the bird called a *Siskin* or *Aberdevine*.

The small branches serve the Highlanders for hurdles, and side-fences to their houses.

And the pliant twigs are well known to answer the purposes of cleanliness, and correction.

There is yet another use to which this tree is applicable, and which I will beg leave strongly to recommend to my country-men: The vernal sap is well known to have a saccharine quality, capable of making sugar, and a wholesome diuretic wine. This tree is always at hand, and the method of making the wine is simple and easy. I shall subjoin a receipt:

In the beginning of March, while the sap is rising, and before the leaves shoot out, bore holes in the bodies of the larger trees, and put fossets therein, made of elder sticks, with the pith taken out, and then put any vessels under to receive the liquor. If the tree be large, you may tap it in four or five places at a time without hurting it; and thus from several trees you may gain several gallons of juice in a day. If you have not enough in one day, bottle up close what you have, till you get a sufficient quantity for your purpose, but the sooner it is used the better.

Boil the sap as long as any scum rises, skimming it all the time. To every gallon of liquor put four pounds of sugar, and boil it afterwards half an hour, skimming it well; then put it into an open tub to cool, and when cold, tun in into your cask; when it has done working, bung it up close, and keep it three months. Then either bottle it off, or draw it out of the cask after it is a year old.

This is a generous and agreeable liquor, and would be a happy substitute in the room of the poisonous whiskey.

BETULA NANA. *Dwarf Birch.* The leaves of this dye a better yellow than those of the preceding.

In northern climes the catkins and seeds are the principal food of grous, ptarmigans; and the humble Laplander is content with a skin of the rein-deer, and a *substratum* of *dwarf-birch* for his bed.

———— ALNUS. *Alder Tree.* The timber of this tree endures moisture well, and is therefore esteemed for making water-pipes, or any other use where the situation of it must be wet or damp, in which state it turns black like ebony. It is used also by the wheelwright and turner, for making wheels of carts, bowls, spoons, rakes, heels for women's shoes, clogs, pattens, &c. The Highlanders often make chairs of the wood, which are very handsome, and of the colour of mahogany.

The knots furnish a beautiful veined wood for cabinets, and the branches make good charcoal.

The bark will dye yarn of a fuscous colour; and the Laplanders tinge their leathern garments red with saliva after masticating the inner bark.

The Highlanders dye their yarn of a black colour, by boiling it with the bark mixed with copperas,

The leaves have been sometimes used in tanning leather, and sheep will feed on them and the smaller branches.

URTICA DIOICA. *Common Stinging Nettle.* The *Aculei,* or stings of the nettle, have a small bladder at their base, full of a burning corrosive liquor: when touched they excite a blister, attended with a violent itching pain, though the sting does not appear to be tubular, or perforated at the top, nor any visible liquor to be infused into the puncture made by it in the flesh. It seems certain, however, that some of this liquor is insinuated into the wound, though invisibly, since the stings of the dried plant excite no pain.

Nettle-tops in the spring are often boiled and eaten by the common people instead of cabbage-greens.

In Arran and other islands, a rennet is made of a strong decoction of nettles: a quart of salt is put to three pints of the decoction, and bottled up for use. A common spoonful of this liquor will coagulate a large bowl of milk very readily and agreeably.

The stalks of nettles are so like in quality to hemp, that in some parts of Europe and Siberia they have been manufactured into cloth, and paper has been made of them.

The whole plant, particularly the root, is esteemed to be diuretic, and has been recommended in the jaundice and nephritic complaints. It is also reckoned astringent, and of service in all kinds of hœmorrhages, but is at present but little in practice.

The roots boiled with alum will dye yarn of a yellow colour.

The Larvæ, or caterpillars of many species of butterflies, feed on the green plant, and sheep and oxen will readily eat it dried.

Order V. *Myrica.*

MYRICA GALE. *Sweet Willow, and Dutch Myrtle.* The leaves have a bitter taste, and a sweet, agreeable, myrtle-like odour.

In Bute, Arran, and most of the Hebrides, as well as in the Highlands, an infusion of the leaves in the way of tea, is frequently given to children to destroy worms.

In Uist, and other of the Western isles, and in Glenald, and other places of the Highland continent, it is sometimes used instead of hops for brewing beer.

In Isla and Jura the inhabitants garnish their dishes with it, and lay it between their linen, and other garments, to give a fine scent, and to drive away moths.

The Swedes dye their yarn with it of a yellow colour, and sometimes use a strong decoction of it to kill bugs and lice, and to cure the itch.

The cones boiled in water will yield a scum like bees wax, capable of being made into candles, similar to those which the Americans make of the berries of *Myrica cerifera*. Lin. or candle-berry myrtle.

Linnæus, from the smell of the plant, is induced to suspect that *Camphor* might possibly be prepared from it.

Order VI. *Polygamia.*

VALANTIA cruciata. *Cross-wort or Mug-weed.* The plant, particularly the roots, will dye a red colour.

It has an astringent quality, and has been reckoned amongst the vulneraries, but is at present out of use.

PARIETARIA Officinalis. *Pellitory of the Wall.* It has a watery, nitrous, diuretic quality. Three ounces of the juice, taken internally, have been found very serviceable in the stranguary.

The plant laid upon heaps of corn infested with weevils, is said to drive away those destructive insects.

Order VII. *Didynamia.*

GLECOMA hederacea. *Ground Ivy.* It is made into tea, and constitutes the pleasantest beverage for children instead of the foreign tea, and is thought to be antiscorbutic.

PRUNELLA vulgaris. *Self-heal.* It is astringent and vulnerary, but is rarely used at present, except by the common people, who bruise and apply it to fresh wounds, and take it in broths and apozems for spitting of blood, and use it by way of injection in the bloody-flux, and other hemorrhages.

MENTHA arvensis. *Corn Mint.* The plant smells much like the blue part of a decayed cheese.

Linnæus says, that the milk of cows which have fed upon this plant can hardly be made to turn to curds.

———— pulegium. *Pennyroyal.* Distilled it is an excellent cordial for young girls, and assists the operations of nature.

THYMUS serpyllum. *Mother of Thyme.* It has a pleasant aromatic scent, and is esteemed a good nervine. An infusion of it by way of tea is reputed to be an almost infallible cure for that troublesome disorder the Incubus, or night-mare.

BALLOTRA nigra. *Stinking Horehound.* The plant has a strong fœtid smell, and has been sometimes recommended in hysteric cases, but is at present little used.

MARRUBIUM vulgare. *White Horehound.* It has a strong and somewhat musky smell, and bitter taste. It is reputed attenuant and resolvent. An infusion of the leaves in water, sweetened with honey, is recommended in asthmatic and phthisicky complaints, and most other diseases of the breast and lungs.

TEUCRIUM scorodonia. *Wood Sage.* The plant has a bitter quality, and smells like hops, with a little mixture of garlick. In the island of Jersey the inhabitants use it in brewing instead of hops. An infusion of it stands recommended in the dropsy.

BETONICA officinalis. *Wood Betony.* The roots in a small dose have an emetic quality, and the powder of the dried plant is a good errhine, and readily promotes sneezing.

NEPETA cataria. *Cat-mint.* The plant has a bitter taste and strong smell, not unlike pennyroyal.

An infusion of it is reckoned a good cephalic and emmenagogue, being found very efficacious in hysterics and the chlorosis. Cats are extremely fond of this plant, whence the name.

LAMIUM album. *White Archangel, or Dead Nettle.* An infusion of the plant is found a very strong bracer. The young leaves in the spring are boiled and eaten as greens by the common people in Sweden.

———— purbureum. *Red ditto.* This is also eaten in Sweden like the preceding.

EUPHRASIA officinalis. *Eyebright.* It has been reputed good for sore eyes, but the faculty have declared it does more harm than good in applications of that kind, there having been instances of persons rendered almost blind by the use of it. The Highlanders do however still retain the practice of it, by making an infusion of it in milk, and anointing the patient's eyes with a feather dipped in it.

RHINANTHUS crista galli. *Yellow-Rattle, or Cock's Comb.* The seeds, when ripe, rattle in their capsules, and indicate the time of hay-harvest.

It has a bitter and somewhat acrid taste, but is eaten by cattle.

MELAMPYRUM pratense. *Meadow Cow-wheat.* Linnæus tells us, that where this plant abounds the yellowest and best butter is made.

DIGITALIS purpurea. *Purple Foxglove.* The plant has a bitter quality.; six or seven spoonsful of the decoction are a strong emetic and cathartic. It has been found serviceable in scrophulous cases, taken internally for some time, and the bruised leaves for an ointment applied outwardly; it is used now in dropsy and consumption.

SCROPHULARIA nodosa. *Knobby-rooted Fig-wort.* The leaves have a fœtid smell, and bitter taste. A decoction of them is said to cure hogs of the mange.

An ointment made of the root has been formerly used to cure the piles and scrophulous sores, but is at present out of practice.

ANTIRRHINUM linaria. *Common Yellow Toad-flax.* An ointment made of the leaves stands recommended as a cure for the piles.

PEDICULARIS sylvatica et palustris. *Common Marsh and Dwarf Louse-wort.* These plants are rarely eaten by cattle, but when they are, they are supposed to make them lousy, whence the name.

Class V. *Pentandria.*

Order I. *Monogynia.*

LYTHOSPERMUM officinale. *Gromwell.* Linnæus informs us that the country girls in Sweden paint their faces with the roots.

CYNOGLOSSUM officinale. *Hound's-tongue.* No quadruped except the goat will eat it.

ANAGALLIS arvensis. *Common Pimpernel.* It varies with scarlet and blue flowers, which open at eight o'clock in the morning, and close about noon. Small birds are very fond of the seeds of this plant.

ATROPA belladonna. *Deadly Nightshade.* The berries of this plant are of a malignant poisonous nature, and, being of a sweet taste, have frequently been destructive to children. A large glass of warm vinegar, taken as soon as possible after eating the berries, will prevent their bad effects.

PRIMULA veris. *Cowslip. Oxlip. Primrose.* The segments of the flowers within, near the base, are marked with red or saffron-coloured spots, which our poet Shakespeare prettily supposes to be the gifts of the fairy-queens, and to be the source of their sweet odours. He thus introduces a fairy speaking—

> And I serve the fairy-queen,
> To dew her orbs upon the green;
> The cowslips tall her pensioners be,
> In their gold coats spots you see;
> Those be rubies, Fairy favours,
> In those freckles live their savours:
> I must go seek some dew-drops here and there,
> And hang a pearl in every cowslip's ear.
>
> MIDSUMMER NIGHT'S DREAM, ACT 2, Sc. 1.

HYOSCYAMUS niger. *Common Henbane.* The whole plant is covered with unctuous fœtid hairs: the flowers are yellow, reticulated with violet-coloured veins. The root, leaves, and seed, are a most powerful narcotic: a few of the seeds have been known to deprive a man of his reason and limbs.

RHAMNUS catharticus. *Buckthorn.* The juice of the berries, in the quantity of five or six drachms, is a strong purge; but it is generally made into a syrup for this purpose, two ounces of which is a dose. The bark is emetic. The juice of the unripe berries with alum, dyes a yellow colour; of the ripe ones, a green colour. The bark also dyes yellow.

Order II. *Digynia.*

CUSCUTA europæa. *Dodder.* It is a parasitical plant of a very singular nature, destitute of leaves and roots.

It consists only of red, succulent, thread-like stalks, twisting about the plant on which it grows in a spiral direction, contrary to the sun's motion, and drawing its nourishment from it by small sucking papillæ, fixed into the pores of the bark or rind, thereby exhausting the foster-plant of its juices, imbibing its virtues, and often destroying it.

GENTIANA. *Gentian.* All the Gentians are esteemed to be good stomachic bitters, and are recommended in the ague, and to strengthen the stomach.

Linnæus informs us that the poor people in Sweden use the *cam* *pestris*, instead of hops, to brew their ale with.

SALSOLA KALI. *Prickly Glass-wort.* The ashes of this plant abound with alkaline salts. One species of the genus (the S *soda*) is much used upon the coasts of the Mediterranean in making pot-ash, soap, and glass. The term alkali originally took its rise from the salts extracted from the ashes of this last mentioned herb, which was called by the Arabic chemists and physicians, KALI.

CHENOPODIUM BONUS HENRICUS. *English Mercury, Wild Spinach, or All Good.* The young leaves in the Spring are often eaten as greens, and are very good tasted.

——————————— ALBUM. *Frost Blite.* In Isla the poor people boil and eat it as greens.

——————————— VIRIDE. *Green Blite.* Eaten as the last.

BETA MARITIMA. *Sea Beet.* The young leaves boiled are wholesome and good greens.

UMBELLIFEROUS PLANTS.

ERYNGIUM MARITIMUM. *Sea Holly or Eryngo.* The young tender shoots, when blanched, may be eaten like asparagus. *Lin. Fl. Suec.*

SANICULA EUROPÆA. *Sanicle.* It has long been esteemed as an astringent and vulnerary, both in external and internal applications.

ŒNANTHE CROCATA. *Hemlock Dropwort.* The roots and leaves of this plant are a terrible poison; several persons have perished by eating it through mistake, either for water-parsneps or for celery, which last it resembles pretty much in its leaves. So extremely deleterious is its nature, that I remember to have heard the late Mr. Christopher D. Ehret, that celebrated botanic painter, say, that while he was drawing this plant, the smell or effluvia only rendered him so giddy, that he was several times obliged to quit the room, and walk out in the fresh air to recover himself; but recollecting at last what might probably be the cause of his repeated illness, he opened the door and windows of the room, and the free air then enabled him

to finish his work without any more returns of his giddi-
ness.

I have seen a large spoonful of the juice of this plant given to a
dog, which made him very sick and stupid, but in about an
hour he recovered: and I have seen a goat eat it with impu-
nity.

To those of the human kind, who have been so unfortunate as
to eat any part of this plant, a vomit is the most approved remedy.

ANGELICA sylvestris. *Wild Angelica.* It renders hay ungrate-
ful to cattle.

LIGUSTICUM scoticum. *Scotch Parsley or Lovage.* It is sometimes eaten raw as a salad, or boiled as greens. The root is
reckoned a good carminative. An infusion of the leaves in
whey they give their calves to purge them.

DAUCUS carota. *Wild Carrot, or Bird's Nest.* The seeds are a
powerful diuretic: an infusion of them in ale or in water as
a tea have been found to give relief in the gravel. The garden
carrot differs from this only by culture.

CONIUM maculatum. *Hemlock.* This plant has certainly narcotic
and poisonous qualities, but notwithstanding this it has lately
been introduced into the Materia Medica, as an excellent medicine to remove almost every complaint arising from obstructions in the glands. The celebrated Stork first brought it
into its present reputation: that gentleman, by many repeated
experiments, found, that an extract, prepared from the fresh
roots in the Spring, was a very powerful and efficacious remedy in almost all kinds of ulcerous, scrophulous, and even
cancerous disorders.

HERACLEUM spondylium. *Cow Parsnep.* Gmelin, in his Flor.
Sibirica, p. 214. tells us, that the inhabitants of Kamtschatka,
about the beginning of July, collect the footstalks of the radical leaves of this plant, and after peeling off the rind, dry
them separately in the sun, and then tying them in bundles
they lay them up carefully in the shade: in a short time afterwards these dried stalks are covered over with a yellow
saccharine efflorescence, tasting like liquorice, and in this
state they are eaten as a great delicacy.

The Russians, not content with eating the stalks thus prepared, contrive to get a very intoxicating spirit from them, by first fermenting them in water with the greater *Bilberries*, (*Vaccinium uliginosum*) and then distilling the liquor to what degree of strength they please, which Gmelin says is more agreeable to the taste than spirits made from corn. This may therefore prove a good succedaneum for whiskey, and prevent the consumption of much barley, which ought to be applied to better purposes. Swine and rabbits are very fond of this plant. In the county of Norfolk it is called *Hog-weed*.

ATHAMANTA meum. *Spignel, Meu.* The root has a warm spicy taste, and is sometimes used in medicine as a carminative and diuretic.

BUNIUM bulbocastanum. *Earth Nut, or Pig Nut.* The roots are bulbous, and taste like a chesnut, whence the trivial name of *Bulbocastanum*. Many persons are fond of them, and in some parts of England they boil them in broth, and serve them up to table.

CRITHMUM maritimum. *Samphire.* The leaves of this plant are used in England as a well known pickle, of a warm aromatic flavour.

IMPERATORIA ostruthium. *Masterwort.* The root is warm and aromatic, and is esteemed a good sudorific. There are recorded instances of its curing the ague, when the bark has failed. It should be dug up in the winter, and a strong infusion made in wine.

ÆTHUSA cynapium. *Lesser Hemlock, or Fool's Parsley.* The plant when bruised has a strong virulent smell, something like garlick. Its qualities correspond to the smell, for it is of a poisonous nature, producing stupors, vomitings, and convulsions. Cooks therefore cannot be too careful that they mistake it not for parsley, which it a good deal resembles.

PHELLANDRIUM aquaticum. *Water Hemlock.* Linnæus informs us that the horses in Sweden, by eating this plant, are seized with a kind of palsy, which he supposes is brought upon them not so much by any noxious qualities in the plant itself, as by a certain insect which breeds in the stalks, called by him, for that reason, Curculeo paraplecticus. Syst. Nat. 610. Purging and bleeding is the best remedy.

CICUTA virosa. *Long-leaved Water Hemlock.* Of the few vegetable poisons in Great Britain this is one of the principal. It is destructive not only to man, but according to most writers on the subject, to almost every beast, except perhaps the goat, which is said to devour it as a grateful food.

—— viride licet pinguescere sæpe cicuta,
Barbigeras pecudes, hominique est acre venenum.

Lucret.

Linnæus assures us that he has known cattle to die by eating the roots; and Webfer informs us, that one ounce of it threw a dog into convulsions, and two ounces killed it : he mentions also its direful effects upon several other animals. And Schwenke, a German writer, gives an account of four boys, who had the misfortune to eat of it ; three of whom died in convulsions. Strong emetics, administered as soon as possible are the most approved antidote.

ÆGOPODIUM PODAGRARIA. *Gout-weed.* The young leaves in the spring, are eaten in Sweden and Switzerland as greens.

CARUM CARUI. *Caraways.* The seeds are a well-known carminative. The young leaves are good in soups, and the roots are by some esteemed a delicate food.

Order III. *Trigynia.*

SAMBUCUS EBULUS. *Dwarf Elder.* The roots are a powerful diuretic : a decoction of them has been found serviceable in the dropsy.

———— NIGRA. *Common Elder.* An infusion of the inner green bark of this shrub in white wine, or its expressed juice to the quantity of half an ounce, or an ounce, is said to prove a moderate cathartic, and in small doses to be an efficacious deobstruent. The bruised leaves in a cataplasm are sometimes applied outwardly in erysipelas and pleurisies, and are reckoned to be very relaxing. The dried flowers are a sudorific, and the juice of the berries, inspissated to the consistence of a rob, proves a safe and useful aperient medicine, good in obstructions of the viscera, and to promote the natural evacuations. The berries are also used to make a wine, which has something of the flavour of frontiniac ; and in some countries they dye cloth of a brown colour with them. The young umbels before the flowers expand are by some esteemed for pickling.

Order V. *Pentagynia.*

LINUM ᴜꜱɪᴛᴀᴛɪꜱꜱɪᴍᴜᴍ. *Flax.* Not to mention the great economical use of this plant in making of linen, the seeds are esteemed an excellent emollient and anodyne : they are used externally in cataplasms, to assuage the pain of inflamed tumours : internally, a slight infusion of linseed, by way of tea, is recommended in coughs as an excellent pectoral, and of great service in pleurisies, and nephritic complaints.

———— ᴄᴀᴛʜᴀʀᴛɪᴄᴜᴍ. *Purging Flax.* A drachm of the dried plant pulverized, or an infusion of a handful of it in whey or water, is a safe purge.

Order IX. *Monœcia.*

BRYONIA ᴀʟʙᴀ. *White Bryony.* The roots are very large, white, and branched, and by the help of moulds, have been formed into human shape, and exhibited to the ignorant for mandrakes.

The whole plant is strongly purgative. The root is bitter, acrid, fœtid, and nauseous. One drachm of it is the common dose ; two drachms have been given to dropsical persons with good success, but it is rarely prescribed in the present practice.

Order X. *Diœcia.*

HUMULUS ʟᴜᴘᴜʟᴜꜱ. *Hops.* The young shoots boiled, and eaten in the Spring, like asparagus, are by many reckoned a delicacy. The hops themselves are bitter and aromatic; a strong decoction of them is esteemed a powerful lithrontriptic ; but their principal use is in brewing ale, to prevent its turning sour.

Order XI. *Syngenesia.*

LEONTODON ᴛᴀʀᴀxᴀᴄᴜᴍ. *Dandelion.* The plant has a bitter milky juice, and a remarkable diuretic quality.

The young leaves in the spring, when blanched and tender, are admired by many as a salad. They are recommended thus taken for the jaundice and gravel.

———————— ᴀᴜᴛᴜᴍɴᴀʟᴇ. *Yellow ditto.* The flower opens about seven o'clock in the morning, and closes at three in the afternoon.

SONCHUS OLERACEUS. *Common Sow-thistle*. The young tender leaves of sow-thistle are in some countries boiled and eaten as greens. They are of a cooling nature, and applied outwardly, by way of cataplasm, have been found serviceable in inflammatory swellings and carbuncles. Swine, hares, and rabbits are fond of them.

The flowers open about six or seven o'clock in the morning, and shut up again at eleven or twelve.

LACTUCA VIROSA. *Strong-scented Wild Lettuce*. The whole plant is full of a bitter milky juice, which when dry is inflammable, and not inferior to opium in its virtues. The leaves are narcotic, and if eaten will intoxicate, which has occasioned it to be called poisonous, and men have from thence been frighted from the use of it; but it is a very gentle and safe opiate. The best way of giving it is in a syrup made from a decoction of the fresh leaves and stalk. In this way it is said to be much preferable to the common diacodium, and may be given to tender constitutions with more safety.

LAPSANA COMMUNIS. *Nipple-wort*. The young leaves in the spring have the taste of radishes, and are eaten by the inhabitants of Constantinople raw as a salad. In some parts of England the common people boil them as greens, but they have a bitter and not agreeable taste.

TRAGOPOGON PRATENSE. *Yellow Goat's-beard*. If the weather be fair, the flowers of this plant open at the rising of the sun, and close again between nine and ten o'clock in the morning. They ripen their seeds in three weeks from the first expansion. The roots are esculent, being boiled and served up to table in the manner of asparagus. The spring shoots are also eaten by some in the same manner. But that which is cultivated in gardens for culinary purposes is generally another species, the *Tragopogon porrifolium*, Lin. commonly called by the gardeners *Salsafy*.

ARCTIUM LAPPA. *Burdock*. This plant, though generally neglected, is capable of being applied to many uses,—the root and stalks are esculent and nutritive : the stalks for this purpose should be cut before the plant flowers, the rind peeled off, and then boiled and served up in the manner of cardoons, or eaten raw as a salad with oil and vinegar,

It is likewise used in medicine: the great Boerhaave recom. mends a decoction of it in pleurisies, peripneumonies, and malignant fevers. An elixir of it has been much extolled for the gout; and an emulsion of the seeds has a powerful diuretic quality. Outwardly applied the leaves have been found serviceable in headachs, the gout, and œdematous swellings.

Cattle refuse to eat it: but sheep propagate it by conveying the seeds from place to place in their wool.

ONOPORDUM Acanthium. *Cotton Thistle.* The receptacles of the flowers, and the tender stalks peeled and boiled, may be eaten in the same manner as artichokes and cardoons.

CARDUUS nutans. *Musk Thistle.* The dried flowers of this and the *Carduus lanceolatus* are used in some countries as a rennet to curdle milk.

Many kinds of Phalænæ are fond of the flowers, and hover over them at night.

————— palustris. *Marsh Thistle.* The tender stalk of this and most of the thistles are esculent, being first peeled and boiled. In this manner the inhabitants of Smoland in Sweden, as Linnæus informs us, often eat them.

————— marianus. *Milk Thistle.* The tender leaves stripped of their spines, are by some boiled and eaten as garden-stuff.

An emulsion of the seeds has sometimes been used to thin the blood, and also to cure pleurisies, but at present is rarely practised.

————— eriophorus. *Woolly-headed Thistle.* The receptacles are pulpous and esculent, like those of the artichoke.

SERRATULA tinctoria. *Saw-wort.* It dyes cloth of an exceeding fine yellow colour, preferable to the *Luteola* or *Genista;* and the colour stands well when fixed with alum.

Cattle are observed to leave this plant untouched.

————— arvensis. *Common Way Thistle.* The plant when burnt yields good ashes for glass-making.

EUPATORIUM cannabinum. *Hemp-Agrimony.* The plant has a very bitter taste. A decoction of the roots operates as a violent emetic and cathartic, and is sometimes taken by the lower class of people to cure the jaundice, dropsy, and cachexy, but it is a rough medicine, and ought to be used with caution. The great Boerhaave made use of an infusion of this plant to foment ulcers and putrid sores. Tournefort informs us, that the Turks cure the scurvy with it. An ounce of the juice, or a drachm of the extract, is a dose.

BIDENS TRIPARTITA. *Trifid Water-Hemp-Agrimony.* A decoction of this plant with alum dyes yarn with a yellow colour. The yarn must be first steeped in alum-water, then dried and steeped in a decoction of the plant, and afterwards boiled in the decoction.

The seeds have been known sometimes to destroy the Cyprinus auratus, or *gold fish*, by adhering to their gills and jaws.

TANACETUM VULGARE. *Common Tansy.* It has a bitter taste and aromatic smell. It is esteemed good to warm and strengthen the stomach, for which reason the young leaves in the spring have received a place among the culinary herbs, their juice being an ingredient in puddings, tansies, and other dainties. It is rarely used in medicine, though extolled as a good emmenagogue. A drachm of the dried flowers has been found very beneficial in hysterics arising from suppressions. The seeds and leaves were formerly in considerable esteem for destroying worms in children, and are reckoned good in colics and flatulencies. In some parts of Sweden and Lapland a bath with a decoction of this plant is made use of to assist in parturition.

CONYZA SQUARROSA. *Plowman's Spikenard.* The plant has an aromatic smell.

ANTHEMIS COTULA. *Stinking Camomile.* The whole plant has a strong fœtid smell, and, where it abounds, is often found to blister the hands of weeders and reapers.

ACHILLEA PTARMICA. *Sneeze-wort.* The plant has an acrid biting taste, and has sometimes been used as an errhine to promote sneezing, and to cure the tooth-ach, by drawing away the rheum from the jaws; but at present it is out of practice. Cattle will readily eat it.

————— MILLEFOLIUM. *Yarrow.* The plant has an astringent quality and is reckoned good to stop all kinds of hœmorrhages, and to heal wounds, but is out of use in the present practice. The Highlanders still continue to make an ointment it to heal and dry up wounds. The common people, in order to cure the headach, do sometimes thrust a leaf of it up their nostrils, to make their nose bleed ; an old practice, which gave rise to one of its English names.

Linnæus informs us, that the inhabitants of Dalekarlia, in Sweden, mix it with their ale instead of hops, and that it gives the liquor an intoxicating quality.

Cattle do not refuse to eat it.

BELLIS PERENNIS. *Common Daisie.* The taste of the leaves is somewhat acid, and in scarcity of garden-stuff, they have in some countries been substituted as a pot-herb. It is at present not used in medicine.

DORONICUM PARDALIANCHES. *Wolf's Bane.* Many writers have supposed the root to be poisonous, and that it would destroy wolves, dogs, and other animals.

INULA HELENIUM. *Elecampane.* The root is acrid, bitter, and aromatic : a conserve of it stands recommended in asthmas, and other disorders of the breast and lungs, as good to promote expectoration. The decoction of it in water, or an infusion in wine, or a spirituous extract, are also extolled as a stomachic and sudorific, and are therefore prescribed in crudities of the stomach, bad digestions, the hypochondria, and contagious diseases. Outwardly applied, a decoction of it is said to cure the itch. Bruised and macerated in urine, with balls of ashes and wortle berries, it dies a blue colour.

MATRICARIA PARTHENIUM. *Feverfew.* The whole plant has a strong fragrant smell, and has always been esteemed a good emmenagogue, and very serviceable in hysteric complaints. The best way of taking it is in a slight infusion in the manner of tea. It is also an agreeable carminative and bitter, strengthens the stomach, and disperses flatulencies. The expressed juice is said to kill worms in the bowels. It has likewise been recommended as a febrifuge, whence it took its English name.

———————— CHAMOMILLA. *Camomile.* The flowers are reckoned antiseptic, and approach in quality to the Peruvian bark. Twenty or thirty grains of them readily promote sweat, and are recommended as a cure for the ague ; and, mixed with salt of wormwood, as excellent in fevers. A decoction of them is esteemed good in nephritic complaints, and to assuage the pains of the colic and dysentery. Baths, lysters, and cataplasms of them are also used in the last intentions. A blue essential oil is obtained by distillation from the flowers, which is supposed to contain all their virtues.

CHRYSANTHEMUM segetum. *Corn Marygold.* These golden flowers turn towards the sun all day, an ornament to the corn-fields, and afford a pleasing sight to the passenger, but are so very detrimental to the husbandman, that a law is in force in Denmark, which obliges the inhabitants every where to eradicate them out of their grounds.

This noxious weed is said to be destroyed by dunging the soil where it grows in the autumn, by letting it lie fallow one summer, and by harrowing the ground in about five days after sowing the seeds for the future crop. Lin. Fl. Suet. 762.

SOLIDAGO virgaurea. *Golden Rod.* The leaves have an astringent and bitter taste, and are esteemed as a good vulnerary and diuretic: they are recommended in the stone and gravel, and in ulcers of the kidneys and bladder, three drachms of the powder being taken every eighth hour.

SENECIO vulgaris. *Common Groundsel.* A strong infusion of this plant acts as an emetic. The Highlanders use it externally in cataplasms as a cooler, and to bring on suppurations. Finches and other small birds are fond of the seeds.

————— aquatica. *Water Ragwort.* The leaves of these plants have a bitter and somewhat acrid taste: a decoction of them will dye green, but the colour does not stand well.

TUSSILAGO farfara. *Common Colt's-foot.* The leaves smoaked in the manner of tobacco, or a syrup or decoction of them and the flowers, stand recommended in coughs and other disorders of the breast and lungs. Practice, however, seems almost to have rejected it.

A kind of tinder or touchwood is in some countries made of the roots, or the downy substance which adheres to them.

————— petasites. *Common Butter-bur.* The leaves of these are the largest of any native plant in Great Britain, and in heavy rains are frequently observed to afford a seasonable shelter to poultry and other small animals.

The root dug up in the spring is resinous, and aromatic. A drachm of it in a dose has been sometimes given as a sudorific alexipharmic, but as it possesses those virtues but in a small degree, it has lost its reputation in the shops.

CENTAUREA CYANUS. *Blue-bottles.* The neutral florets infused in water, or any spirituous liquor, give it a beautiful blue colour, which being mixed with an acid, turns red; with an alkali, green; a fine colour is also prepared from them for the use of painting, by drying them first into cakes, in an hair-sieve in an oven, after the manner of drying saffron. See Gentleman's Magazine, 1748, March.

The Swedes mix them with tobacco, but more for colour than taste.

A water distilled from them was formerly recommended in inflammations of the eyes, but is now disused.

CENTAUREA SCABIOSA. *Great Knap-weed.* It varies sometimes with white flowers. The seeds are a winter food to small birds.

JASIONE MONTANA. *Hairy Sheep's Scabious.* Linnæus says that bees are fond of the flowers.

VIOLA ODORATA. *Sweet Violet.* The flowers are esteemed to be anodyne, cooling, and emollient. A syrup made of them proves an agreeable and useful laxative to children: the leaves are also emollient, and the seeds diuretic.

The blue tincture of the violets is a common test of all acids and alkaline substances, for being mixed the first will always turn it of a red colour, the latter of a green.

The urks make a violet sugar of the flowers, which dissolved in water makes their favourite liquor called Sorbet. Hasselquist's Voyage, p. 254.

The Caledonian ladies formerly used them as a cosmetic, as appears from the advice given in the following Gaulic lines:

Sail-chuach as bianne ghabhar
Suadh re t aghaidh,
'Scha 'n'eil mac ri'air an domhan
Nach bi air do dheadhai'.
Thus translated,

" Anoint thy face with goat's milk in which violets have been
" infused, and there is not a young prince upon earth who
" would not be charmed with thy beauty."

—— TRICOLOR. *Pansies or Heart's Ease.* In Warwickshire and Worcestershire this plant is called by the common people *Love in Idleness,* and therefore is doubtless the herb to which the inventive fancy of Shakespeare attributes such extraordinary virtues in the person of Oberon king of the fairies, in the Midsummer Night's Dream. Act 2. Sc. 2.

Yet mark'd I where the bolt of Cupid fell,
It fell upon a little western flower,
Before milk white, now purple with love's wound,
And maidens call it *Love in Idleness.*
Fetch me that flower, the herb I shew'd thee once;
The juice of it, on sleeping eye-lids laid,
Will make or man or woman madly doat
Upon the next live creature that it sees.

Class VI. *Hexandria.*

SIX STAMINA.

Order I. *Monogynia.*

BERBERIS vulgaris. *Barberry-bush.* The fruit is cooling, and good to quench thirst in fevers, for which purpose it is generally made into a conserve.

The inner bark, steeped in white wine, is purgative, and has been found often to be very serviceable in the jaundice.

ALLIUM ursinum. *Ramsons.* If cows happen to feed upon it, the garlick odour will be communicated to the milk, butter, and cheese.

The inhabitants of Arran take an infusion of the leaves for the gravel with good success.

HYACINTHUS non scriptus. *Harebell.* The Highlanders call this plant in their language Fuath-muc, i. e. *The aversion of Swine,* and say that swine have a particular dislike to the roots.

JUNCUS conglomeratus. *Cluster-flowered Rush.* This rush is used to make wicks for candles, and the pith of it to make toy-baskets.

————— effusus. *Common Soft Rush.* This is likewise used for making candle-wicks, and in some places for ropes and baskets.

Order II. *Trigynia.*

COLCHICUM autumnale. *Meadow Saffron.* An oxymel prepared from the roots, gathered in the beginning of the Summer, and administered in the quantity of six drachms to a boy, and an

ounce and a half to a man, by a drachm at a dose, three or
four times a day, has, in several instances, been found to cure
the dropsy, but in more has failed.

TRIGLOCHIN PALUSTRE. *Arrow-headed Grass.*

———————— MARITIMUM. *Sea-spiked Grass.* Cattle are very
fond of both these.

RUMEX ACUTUS. *Sharp-pointed Dock.* A decoction of the root,
taken internally, is recommended against the scurvy, and
other cutaneous disorders.

———————— AQUATICUS. *Great Water Dock.* The root in decoction or
essence is esteemed an excellent antiscorbutic, and pulverized
is reckoned a good dentifrice.

———————— ACETOSA. *Common Sorrel.* The Laplanders boil a large
quantity of the leaves in water, and mix the juice, when cold,
in the milk of the rein-deers, which they esteem an agreeable and wholesome food, and which will keep in a cool place
for a long while.

The leaves are an agreeable acid, and are reckoned a good antiscorbutic.

Order IV. *Diadelphia.*

FUMARIA OFFICINALIS. *Officinal Fumitory.* The plant has a bitter
taste, and is used in medicine as a great purifier of the blood,
in the decline, hypochondria, and scurvy. The great *Boerhaave* frequently prescribed it in the black jaundice and bilious
colics: a drachm of the extract or inspissated juice is the
common dose.

Order VIII. *Tetradynamia.*

CRAMBE MARITIMA. *Sea Cole-wort.* The young leaves, covered up
with sand and blanched while growing, are boiled and eaten
as a great delicacy.

SUBULARIA AQUATICA. *Awl-wort.* It is very remarkable, that
this diminutive plant flowers under the water; whereas most
other aquatic vegetables emerge from that element at the time
of flowering. This power of emergence seems however the
less necessary in this plant, as the petals are scarcely ever
seen to expand, but connive together, so as most probably to
defend the impregnating *Pollen* from the injuries of the water.

THLASPI ARVENSE. *Treacle Mustard.* The plant smells of garlick, and in countries where it abounds, is found often to communicate its disagreeable odour to the milk of cows that feed on it. The seeds abound with an oil, used formerly for the rheumatism and sciatica, but at present is out of practice.

COCHLEARIA OFFICINALIS. *Officinal Scurvy-grass.* It has an acrid, bitter, and acid taste, and is highly recommended for the scurvy. There are instances of a whole ship's crew having been cured of that distemper by it; and as it abounds with acid salts, there can be no doubt but that it is a great resister of putrefaction. The best way of taking it is raw in a salad. It is also diuretic, and useful in dropsies. The Highlanders esteem it as a good stomachic.

LEPIDIUM LATIFOLIUM. *Pepper-wort.* The young leaves are eaten sometimes in salads; they have a pungent acrid taste, and are reckoned *antiscorbutic.*

CARDAMINE HIRSUTA. *Hirsute Ladies-smock.* The young leaves are a good salad.

———— PRATENSIS. *Cuckow-flower.* The leaves are very acrid, and the flowers have lately had some repute in the cure of epileptic fits.

———— AMARA. *Bitter-cress.* The young leaves are acrid and bitterish, but do not taste amiss in salads.

SISYMBRIUM NASTURTIUM. *Water-cresses.* The young leaves are well known to furnish an agreeable salad, and have always been esteemed as an excellent *antiscorbutic:* they are said likewise to be beneficial in removing obstructions of the viscera, and in the jaundice.

ERYSIMUM ALLIARIA. *Sauce-alone.* The leaves were formerly in use for seasoning savoury dishes, but are at present little regarded, the different kinds of *Allium* being esteemed much more preferable.

An outward application of them is recommended by *Boerhaave,* and others, in gangreens and cancerous ulcers.

SINAPIS ARVENSIS. *Wild Mustard.* The young plants, before they flower, are boiled and eaten as greens in several parts of *England.*

———— ALBA. *White Mustard.* The seminal leaves of this plant, with those of the *Lepidium sativum Lin.* afford a well-known salad in the spring.

SINAPIS nigra. *Common Mustard.* The leaves in the spring are in some parts of *England* boiled and eaten as greens.

The seeds are well known for culinary uses, and are sometimes used externally in medicine, where irritation is intended without blistering.

BRASSICA napus. *Wild Navew.* There is a variety of this, which has an esculent root, and which is cultivated in many parts of *Europe* for the sake of an oil which is pressed from the seeds.

Class VIII. *Octandria.*

EIGHT STAMINA.

Order I. *Monogynia.*

VACCINIUM myrtillus. *Whortle-berries, or Bill-berries.* The berries have an astringent quality. In *Arran* and the western isles they are given in diarrhœas and dysenteries with good effect.

The *Highlanders* frequently eat them in milk, which is a cooling agreeable food, and sometimes they make them into tarts and jellies, which last they mix with *Whiskey* to give it a relish to strangers.

They dye a violet colour, but it requires to be fixed with alum. The grous feed upon them in the autumn.

——— vitis idæa. *Red Whortle-berries.* The berries have an acid cooling quality, useful to quench the thirst in fevers. The *Swedes* are very fond of them made into the form of a rob or jelly, which they eat with their meat as an agreeable acid, proper to correct the animal alkali.

EPILOBIUM angustifolium. *Rosebay Willow-herb.* An infusion of the leaves of this plant has an intoxicating quality, as the inhabitants of *Kamtschatka* have learnt, who likewise eat the white young shoots, which creep under the ground, and brew a sort of ale from the dried pith of it.

The down of the seeds has lately been manufactured by mixing it with cotton or beaver's hair.

ERICA cinerea. *Fine-leaved Heath.* Heath or Hather is applied to many œconomical purposes amongst the Highlanders: they frequently cover their houses with it instead of thatch, or else twist it into ropes, and bind down the thatch with them in a

kind of lattice-work : in most of the Western isles they dye
their yarn of a yellow colour, by boiling it in water with the
green tops and flowers of this plant: in Rum, Skye, and the
Long-Island, they frequently tan their leather in a strong decoction of it : formerly the young tops are said to have been
used alone to brew a kind of ale, and even now it is reported that the inhabitants of Isla and Jura still continue to
brew a very potable liquor by mixing two-thirds of the tops
of hather to one-third of malt. This is not the only refreshment that hather affords : the hardy Highlanders frequently
make their beds with it, laying the roots downwards, and the
tops upwards; which, though not quite so soft and luxurious
as beds of down, are altogether as refreshing to those who
sleep on them, and perhaps much more healthy.

DAPHNE LAUREOLA. *Spurge Laurel.* It is extremely acrid and
caustic, and therefore rarely used in the present practice.

Order III. *Trigynia.*

POLYGONIUM BISTORTA. *Great Bistort.* The root has an acid
austere taste, and is a powerful astringent : the leaves are by
some boiled in the spring, and eaten as greens.

————————— VIVIPARUM. *Small Bistort.* The inhabitants of
Kamtschatka, and sometimes the Norwegians, when pressed
with hunger, feed upon the roots of this plant.

————————— PERSICARIA. *Spotted Bistort.* A decoction of the
plant with alum dyes a yellow colour.

————————— HYDROPIPER. *Water Pepper.* It is a diuretic, but
seldom used. A decoction of it dyes a yellow colour.

Order V. *Diadelphia.*

POLYGALA VULGARIS. *Milk-wort.* It has a bitter taste, and has
been found to possess much the same virtues as the Polygala
Senega, from *America*. It purges without danger. It is also
emetic and diuretic, and sometimes acts in the three different
ways together. A spoonful of the decoction, made by boiling an ounce of the herb in a pint of water till half is ex-
haled, has been found serviceable in pleurisies and fevers, by
promoting a diaphoresis and expectoration ; and three spoonsful of the same, taken once an hour, have proved beneficial

in the dropsy and anasarca. It has also been found successful in phthisicky complaints.

Order VI. *Monœcia.*

QUERCUS ROBUR. *Common Oak.* The oak is remarkable for its slowness of growth, bulk, and longevity. It has been remarked that the trunk has attained to the size only of fourteen inches in diameter, and of some to twenty, in the space of fourscore years.

As to bulk, we have account of an oak belonging to Lord Powis, growing in Bromfield wood, near Ludlow, in Shropshire, in the year 1764, the trunk of which measured 68 feet in girth, 23 in length, and which, reckoning 90 feet for the larger branches, contained in the whole 1455 feet of timber, round measure, or 29 loads and five feet, at 50 feet to a load.

And, with respect to longevity, Linnæus gives account of an oak 260 years old; but we have had some traditions of some in England (how far to be depended upon we know not) that have attained to more than double that age.

Besides the grand purposes to which the timber is applied in navigation and architecture, and the bark in tanning of leather, there are other uses, of less consequence, to which the different parts of this tree have been referred.

The Highlanders use the bark to dye their yarn of a brown colour, or, mixed with copperas, of a black colour. They call the oak "The king of all the trees in the forest," and the herdsman would think himself and his flock unfortunate if he had not a staff of it.

The saw-dust from the timber, and even the leaves of the tree, have been found capable of tanning, though much inferior to the bark for that purpose

So great is the astringency of the bark, that in a larger dose, like the Peruvian kind, it has been known to cure the ague.

The expressed juice of the galls or oak-apples (excrescences occasioned by a small insect called a Cynips) mixed with vitriol and gum-arabic, makes ink.

The leaves of the oak are very subject to be covered with a sweet viscous juice, called honey-dew, which bees and other insects are very fond of. The leaves of a great variety of Phalenæ also feed upon them.

The acorns are a good food to fatten swine and turkies; and, after the severe winter of the year 1709, the poor people in France were miserably constrained to eat them themselves. There are, however, acorns produced from another tree (the Spanish Chesnut), which are eaten to this day in Spain and Greece, with as much pleasure as chesnuts, without the dreadful compulsion of hunger; agreeably to what Ovid has delivered of the Golden Age:

> Contentiq; cibis nullo cogente creatis,
> Arbuteos fœtus, montanaq; fraga legebant,
> Cornaq; & in duris hærentia moro rubetis,
> Et quæ deciderant patula Jovis arbore glandes.
>
> *Ovid. Met. Lib.* 1, *v.* 103.

CORYLUS AVELLANA. *Hazel-nut Tree.* The kernels of the fruit have a mild, farinaceous, oily taste, agreeable to most palates. Squirrels and mice are fond of them, and some birds, such as jays, nutcrackers, &c. A kind of chocolate has been prepared from them, and there are instances of their having been formed into bread. The oil expressed from them is little inferior to the oil of almonds, and is used by painters, and by chemists, for receiving and retaining odours. The charcoal made of the wood is used by painters in drawing.

Some of the Highlanders, where superstition is not totally subsided, look upon the tree itself as unlucky, but are glad to get two of the nuts naturally conjoined, which is a good omen. These they call *Cnò-chomhlaich*, and carry them as an efficacious charm against witchcraft.

CARPINUS BETULUS. *Horn-beam Tree.* The wood is esteemed by the mill-wright and wheel-wright for pullies, axles, shafts, &c. Very neat aspalier hedges, by the sides of garden-walks, are often formed of the young trees: the inner bark will dye yarn of a yellow colour, and cattle are fond of the leaves.

Order VII. *Diœcia.*

RHODIOLA ROSEA. *Rose Root.* The inhabitants of the Farro islands use this plant as a remedy for the scurvy. A cataplasm of the fresh roots applied to the forehead, is said to relieve the head-ach, and to heal malignant ulcers.
The inhabitants of Greenland eat it as garden-stuff.

A fragrant kind of rose-water is capable of being distilled from the roots.

POPULUS ALBA. *White Poplar*. It is a tree of so quick a growth that in some situations it will attain to full maturity in 20 years.

In low moist grounds it is esteemed a good tree to form avenues.

———— TREMULA. *Aspen*. The bark of this tree is green and smooth. The leaves at their first eruption, are hairy above, and cottony underneath, but, when full grown, are smooth, slightly heart-shaped, or nearly round, with a few angular dents on the edges, and supported on long foot-stalks, which are compressed at the top, so that the leaves are perpetually trembling with every breath of wind. At the base of the young leaves are two united glands.

It is a tree of speedy growth. The bark of it is the favourite food of beavers, where those animals are found.

The wood is soft and white, very light and smooth. It is used to make pannels or pack-saddles, wood cans, milk-pails, clogs, pattens, &c.

Horses, sheep, and other animals, will feed on the leaves.

The Highlanders entertain a superstitious notion, that our Saviour's cross was made of this tree, and for that reason suppose that the leaves of it can never rest.

———— NIGRA. *Black Poplar*. It is a tree of quick growth, the trunk naked and lofty, the head regular and beautiful. The wood is light and soft, sometimes used by turners. The buds yield a yellow resinous unquent, formerly used as an emollient and soporific, but is now out of practice.

The indigent inhabitants of Kamtschatka are sometimes reduced to the necessity of converting the inner bark into bread.

Of the cotton down of the seeds paper has been made.

The roots have been observed to dissolve into a kind of gelatinous substance, and to be coated with a tubular crustaceous spar, called by naturalists *Osteocolla*, formerly much esteemed for bringing on a Callus in fractured bones.

Order VIII. *Polygamia*.

ACER PSEUDO-PLATANUS. *Great Maple*. The wood is soft, and used by turners for making bowls, trenchers, and other utensils. The knots are beautifully veined, and desired by the cabinet maker.

The tree itself is very ornamental in avenues, affording an agreeable shade.

By tapping it yields a liquor not unlike that of the birch-tree, from which the Americans make a sugar, and the Highlanders sometimes an agreeable and wholesome wine.

———— CAMPESTRE. *Common Maple.* The wood is used by turners for the same purposes as the foregoing, and sometimes for making gun-stocks.

Class IX. *Enneandria.*

NINE STAMINA.

Order II. *Diœcia.*

MERCURIALIS PERENNIS. *Dog's Mercury.* This plant is of a soporific deleterious nature, noxious both to man and beast. There are instances of those who have eaten it by mistake, instead of *Chenopodium Bonus Henricus*, or English Mercury, and have thereby slept their last sleep.

It is called, in the isle of Skye, *Lus-glen-Bracadale*, and I was informed that it is there sometimes taken by way of infusion to bring on a salivation. How well it answers the intention I know not, but the experiment seems to be dangerous.

Class X. *Decandria.*

Order I. *Monogynia.*

ARBUTUS ALPINA, *Alpine Arbutus.* The berry of a black colour, when ripe, has a taste something resembling that of black currants.

————— UVA URSI. *Bear-berries.* The powder of the leaves taken six or eight mornings in the quantity of half a drachm was not long since a celebrated medicine for the stone and gravel, but is at present rather out of repute.

The whole plant is however found to be very serviceable, by means of its astringent quality, in tanning of leather: and the berries are a food for grous and other game.

Order IV. *Pentagynia.*

SEDUM ACRE. *Pepper Stone-crop.* The juice of it externally is recommended in ulcerous sores and cancers : taken internally it operates strongly as an emetic and cathartic. An ounce of it, boiled in twelve ounces of ale, and taken in four doses, has been found serviceable in the dropsy.

——— FLOS CUCULI. *Cuckow-flower.* Cattle refuse to eat it.

OXALIS ACETOSELLA. *Wood-sorrel.* The leaves are radical only, and numerous ; three grow together at the top of one foot-stalk, heart shaped, hairy, their points all meeting in a centre, and endued with a degree of sensibility, for when struck or handled they droop. Linnæus says they are expanded in moist rainy weather, and contracted in dry.

The whole plant has an agreeable acid taste, and cooling quality, and is recommended in malignant fevers, and for the scurvy. In the island of Arran I was informed that a whey or tea of it was used in putrid and other fevers, with good success.

Order V. and VI. *Monodelphia and Diadelphia.*

GERANIUM SYLVATICUM. *Mountain Crane's-bill.* The flowers are used by the Icelanders to dye a violet colour.

——— ROBERTIANIUM. *Herb Robert.* It is reckoned astringent and vulnerary, but is seldom used in medicine.

It is said that the smell of the bruised herbs will drive away bugs.

FLOWERS PAPILIONACEOUS.

SPARTIUM SCOPARIUM. *Common Broom.* It has a bitter taste and diuretic quality. A *lixivium* made of the ashes, or a decoction of the plant, stands recommended for the dropsy. The flowers and seeds, from two drachms to half an ounce, are a strong vomit. Its œconomical uses are various.

The flower-buds are in some countries pickled and eaten as capers, and the seeds have been made a bad substitute for coffee. The twigs and branches are used for making of brooms, and for tanning of leather, in which intention they are not inferior to oak-bark : they are also used instead of thatch to cover houses : the old wood furnishes the cabinet-maker with most beautiful materials for vaneering : the tender branches are in some places mixed with hops for brewing ;

and the macerated bark is found capable of being manufactured into cloth.

ULEX europœus. *Furze, Whins, or Gorse.* In England fences are frequently made of this plant by sowing the seeds.

Horses, sheep, and other cattle are very fond of it, but as the spines annoy them, and prevent their feeding on it, the husbandmen in many parts of Wales bruise the tender branches, or grind them in mills for that purpose, by which means they become an excellent fodder.

GENISTA tinctoria. *Dyer's-weed.* This plant is well known to dye yarn and cloth with a bright yellow colour.

A salt prepared from the ashes of it is by some recommended in the dropsy.

ONONIS arvensis. *Restharrow or Cammock.* A plant, whose roots are so stubbornly fixed, as to prevent the progress of the harrow. As this plant abounds in the Holy-Land, Haselquist (in his voyage thither, p. 289) supposes, with great probability, that this is the thorn mentioned in the scripture, which the ground produced after the curse. (*Gen.* iii. 18.)

The root and bark have a diuretic quality, and are recommended in the gravel.

TRIFOLIUM officinalis. *Melilot.* The plant has a very peculiar strong scent, and disagreeable bitter acrid taste, but such however as is not displeasing to cattle. The flowers are sweet-scented.

It has generally been esteemed emollient and digestive, and been used in fomentations and cataplasms, particularly in the plaster employed in dressing blisters, but is now laid aside, as its quality is found to be rather acrid and irritating, than emollient or resolvent.

It communicates a most loathsome flavour to wheat and other grain, so as to render it unfit for making bread.

——————— repens. *Dutch Clover.* It is well known to be an excellent fodder for cattle, and the leaves are a good rustic hygrometer, as they are always relaxed and flaccid in dry weather, but erect in moist or rainy.

——————— pratense. *Purple Clover.* It affords a very plentiful fodder to horses and other cattle, but when they feed too greedily on the fresh herb, it blows them up in such a manner with wind, that unless they are speedily relieved by tapping them in the belly, or some other similar operation, they soon perish. In Ireland the poor people, in a scarcity of corn, make a kind of bread of the dried flowers of this and the preceding plant reduced to powder. They call the plant *Chambroch*, and esteem the bread made of it to be very wholesome and nutritive.

TRIFOLIUM AGRARIUM. *Hop Trefoil.* It is an excellent fodder for cattle.

ORNITHOPUS PERPUSILLUS. *Bird's-foot.* The pods are slightly hairy, curved, jointed with six or eight articulations, and terminated with a claw, so that altogether they not unaptly represent a bird's foot. Each joint contains a single seed.

LOTUS CORNICULATUS. *Bird's-foot Trefoil.* It is an excellent fodder for cattle, and would probably be well worth attention in agriculture.

The insect called by Linnæus *Thrips glauca* sometimes renders the flowers tumid and monstrous.

MEDICAGO LUPULINA. *Melilot Trefoil.* It has of late years been cultivated in some parts of England for fodder, but it is probable that the *Lotus corniculatus*, and *Trifolium agrarium* above-mentioned, would turn to a better account.

ANTHYLLIS VULNERARIA. *Kidney-vetch.* The plant is supposed to have an astringent quality, and is scarcely ever eaten by cattle.

ASTRAGALUS GLYCYPHYLLOS. *Wild Liquorice.* The leaves have a sweetish taste, mixed with bitterness. An infusion of them has by some been recommended in suppressions, and for the gravel.

OROBUS TUBEROSUS. *Wood Pease.* The Highlanders have a great esteem for the tubercles of the roots of this plant; they dry and chew them in general to give a better relish to their liquor; they also affirm them to be good against most disorders of the chest, and that by the use of them they are enabled to repel hunger and thirst for a long time. In Breadalbane and Ross-shire they sometimes bruise and steep them in water, and make an agreeable fermented liquor with them. They have a sweet taste, something like the roots of liquorice, and when boiled, we are told, are well flavoured and nutritive, and in times of scarcity have served as a substitute for bread.

VICIA cracca. *Tufted Vetch.* It is reckoned to be a good fodder for cattle.

—— sativa. *Common Vetch or Tare.* It is known to be an excellent fodder for horses: in some parts of England the crop is ploughed in to answer the purposes of manure to the land: pigeons are very fond of the seeds, and in some parts of Sweden, &c. they enter into the composition of bread, either alone, or mixed with the flour of rye. In England a decoction of them in water is sometimes given by nurses to expel the small-pox and measles.

—— sepium. *Bush Vetch.* It is said to be a good fodder for cattle.

LATHYRUS pratensis. *Tare-everlasting.* It is an excellent fodder, and some soils would probably reward the husbandman's cultivation.

The badger is said to feed upon it.

Class XII. *Dodecandria.*

TWELVE TO TWENTY STAMINA.

Order I. *Monogynia.*

LYTHRUM salicaria. *Loosestrife.* It is of an astringent quality, but rarely used in medicine. Cattle are fond of it.

Order II. *Digynia.*

AGRIMONIA eupatoria. *Agrimony.* The leaves make a very pleasant tea, said to be serviceable in hœmorrhages, and in obstructions of the liver and spleen. The country people also use them sometimes by way of cataplasm in contusions and fresh wounds.

Order III. *Trigynia.*

RESEDA luteola. *Wild Woad.* This plant is cultivated and much used for dying woollen and silk of a yellow colour. The fresh herb, shredded and boiled, or dryed and reduced to a powder, are the ways of using it.

EUPHORBIA helioscopia. *Sun-spurge or Wart-spurge.* This

together with the several species are full of a milky juice, which in most is of a hot caustic nature, capable of raising a blister, or burning away warts.

Order IV. *Dodecagynia.*

SEMPERVIVUM tectorum. *Houseleek.* It is recommended as a cooler by way of cataplasm to burns and hot ulcers; and the juice mixed with honey, and laid on with a pencil, has been found of service to cure the *Thrush* in children. Boerhaave found, that ten ounces of the juice, given internally, was beneficial in dysenteries.

Class XII. *Polyandria.*

TWENTY OR MORE STAMINA.

SECT. I. STAMINA INSERTED ON THE RECEPTACLE.

Order I. *Monogynia.*

PAPAVER rhæas. *Red Poppy.* A conserve, infusion, or syrup of the flowers is esteemed as a gentle *Narcotic* and *Anodyne.*

CHELIDONIUM majus. *Celandine.* The whole plant is full of a yellow, bitter, acrid juice, esteemed good in the jaundice and dropsy. It is used outwardly to take away warts, tetters, ringworms, &c. and diluted with rose-water, to take specks and films off the eyes.

TILIA europæa. *Linden or Lime-tree.* The wood is light, smooth, and of a spungy texture, used for making lasts and tables for shoe-makers, &c.

Ropes and bandages are made of the bark, and mats and rustic garments of the inner rind in Carniola, and some other countries.

NYMPHÆA lutea. *Yellow Water-lily.* Linnæus tells us that swine are fond of the leaves and roots of this plant; and that crickets and *blattæ*, or cock-roaches, may be driven out of houses by the smoke in burning of it.

———— alba. *White Water-lily.* The root has an astringent, and bitter taste, like the roots of most aquatic plants that run deep into the mud. The Highlanders make a dye with it, of a dark chesnut colour.

RANUNCULUS FLAMMULA. *Lesser Spear-wort*. It has an acrid and caustic quality, and is used in many parts of the highlands to raise blisters : for this purpose the leaves are well bruised in a mortar, and applied in one or more limpet shells to the part where the blisters are to be raised. This is the practice in the isle of Skye, and other places upon the coast.

——————— FICARIA. *Pile-wort*. The flower opens at nine o'clock in the morning, and closes at five in the evening.

The young leaves in the spring are boiled by the common people in some parts of Sweden, and eaten as greens. The roots are sometimes washed bare by the rains, so that the tubercles appear above ground, and in this state have induced the ignorant, in superstitious times, to fancy that it has rained wheat, which these tubercles do a little resemble. The seeds of this plant commonly prove abortive, but this defect in nature is amply compensated by its remarkable readiness to increase by the granulated roots.

——————— SCELERATUS. *Celery-leaved Crowfoot.* The whole plant has a most acrimonious quality ; if bruised and laid upon any part of the body, it will in a few hours raise a blister. Strolling beggars have been known sometimes purposely t make sores with it, in order the more readily to move compassion.

——————— BULBOSUS. *Butter-cups.* The whole plant is extremely acrid and corrosive, especially the fresh roots, which readily raise a blister, and as safely as *Cantharides ;* and yet notwithstanding this corrosive quality, the roots when boiled become so mild as to be eatable.

——————— ACRIS. *Upright Meadow Crowfoot.* The whole plant is hot and caustic, readily and safely raising a blister, without affecting the urinary passages, by bringing upon the patient a stranguary or the like.

The cattle leave this plant untouched, at least the stalks and flowers of it.

——————— ARVENSIS. *Corn Crowfoot.* The juice of this kind is acrid like the preceding. An ounce of it given to a dog has killed him in three days, the stomach being inflamed, corroded, and blistered.

CALTHA PALUSTRIS. *Marsh Marygold.* The plant has an acrid

quality, but the young flower-buds in some parts of Germany are pickled and sold for capers.

HELLEBORUS viridis. *Green-flowered Hellebore.* A drachm of the leaves reduced to powder is sometimes given to destroy worms.

THALICTRUM flavum. *Meadow Rue.* The root and leaves will dye a yellow colour. Cattle are fond of this plant.

TROLLIUS europœus. *Globe-flower.* The country people in Sweden strew their floors and pavements on holidays with the flowers, which have a pleasant smell, and are ornamental in gardens. Our northern poet makes the young laird wish to gather these flowers to weave a chaplet for his Katy's brow :

> Soon as the clear goodman of day,
>   Bends his morning draught of dew,
> We'll gae to some burn-side to play,
>   And gather flowers to busk ye'r brow.
> We'll 'pon the dasies on the green,
>   The *Lucken Gowans* frae the bog,
> Between hands now and then we'll lean,
>   And sport upon the velvet fog.
> Tea Table Miscellany of Allan Ramsay, in a song called,
>   The Young Laird and Edinburgh Katy.

Order VII. *Monodelphia.*

MALVA sylvestris. *Common Mallow.* The whole plant is mucilaginous and emollient ; a decoction of it, or an infusion of the flowers, is recommended as a pectoral, and good for the stone and gravel, and other complaints in the urinary passages ; it is likewise given in clysters in the dysentery and tenesmus, and is used by way of cataplasm in inflammations : the ancients fed upon a species of mallow, though probably not this kind, as we learn from Horace :

> —————————Me pascunt olivæ,
> Me Cichorea, *levesq; malvæ.* Lib. I. Ode xxx.

ALTHÆA officinalis. *Marsh Mallow.* The roots and leaves have a mucilaginous quality, and are often used in a syrup or decoction as a balsamic pectoral for coughs and hoarsenesses. It is found also to be serviceable in nephritic complaints, and

the strangnary ; and is used in cataplasms and fomentations against swellings. The root will turn water to a jelly.

Order VIII. *Polyadelphia.*

HYPERICUM ANDROSCÉMUM. *Tutsan.* It is a good vulnerary, the
leaves readily healing any fresh wounds, whence it took the
French name of *Tutsan* or *Tout-sain*, i. e. All-heal.

———————— PERFORATUM. *St. John's Wort.* An oil or tincture
of the flowers is esteemed a good vulnerary. The expressed
juice or infusion of the same is reckoned good to destroy
worms, to resolve coagulated blood, and to promote *urine.*

The dried plant boiled in water with alum, dyes yarn of a
yellow colour, and the Swedes give a fine purple tinge to their
spirituous liquors with the flowers.

The superstitious in Scotland carry this plant about them as a
charm against the dire effects of witchcraft or enchantment.
They also cure, or fancy they cure their ropy milk, which
they suppose to be under some malignant influence, by putting
this herb into it, and milking afresh upon it.

Order IX. *Monœcia.*

PINUS SYLVESTRIS. *Scotch Fir.* Few trees have been applied to
more uses than this. The tallest and straightest are formed
by nature for masts to our navy. The timber is resinous,
durable, and applicable to numberless domestic purposes,
such as flooring and wainscoting of rooms, making of beds,
chests, tables, boxes, &c. From the trunk and branches of
this, as well as most others of the pine tribe, tar and pitch is
obtained. By incision, barras, Burgundy pitch, and turpentine, are acquired and prepared. The resinous roots are dug
out of the ground in many parts of the Highlands, and, being
divided into small splinters, are used by the inhabitants to burn
instead of candles. At *Loch-Broom,* in *Ross-shire,* we observed
that the fishermen made ropes of the inner bark ; but hard
necessity has taught the inhabitants of Sweden, Lapland, and
Kamtschatka, to convert the same into bread. To effect this
they, in the Spring season, make choice of the tallest and
fairest trees, then stripping off carefully the outer bark, they
collect the soft, white, succulent, interior bark, and dry it in

the shade. When they have occasion to use it, they first toast
it at the fire, then grind, and, after steeping the flour in warm
water, to take off the resinous taste, they make it into thin
cakes, which are baked for use. On this strange food the
poor inhabitants are sometimes constrained to live for a
whole year; and, we are told, through custom, become at
last even fond of it. *Linnæus* remarks, that this same bark-
bread will fatten swine; and humanity obliges us to wish,
that men might never be reduced to the necessity of robbing
them of such a food.

The interior bark, of which the above-mentioned bread is made,
the Swedish boys frequently peel off the trees in the spring,
and eat raw with greedy appetite.

From the cones of this tree is prepared a diuretic oil, like the
oil of turpentine, and a resinous extract, which has similar
virtues with the balsam of Peru.

An infusion or tea of the buds is highly commended as an antiscorbutic.

The farina, or yellow powder, of the male flowers is sometimes
in the spring carried away by the winds, in such quantities,
where the trees abound, as to alarm the ignorant with the
notion of its raining brimstone.

The trees live to a great age; Linnæus affirms to 400 years.

Order X. *Diœcia.*

TAXUS BACCATA. *Yew-tree.* The wood is red and veined, very hard
and smooth, and much used by turners and cabinet-makers.

The tree is very patient of the shears, and will assume almost
any figure.

It has generally been supposed to have a poisonous quality.
We have repeated accounts of horses and cows that have died
by eating it; but whether the yew was the immediate cause
of their death, is a matter of some doubt.

The berries are certainly not poisonous.

Our ancestors esteemed the wood of this tree as superior to any
other for making bows. For this intent it was planted in
almost every church yard, for the convenience and ready use
of the several parishioners.

SECT. II. STAMINA INSERTED ON THE CALYX OR COROLLA.

PRUNUS PADUS. *Bird-cherry.* The fruit is black when ripe, and of the size of grapes, of a nauseous taste, eaten in Sweden and Kamtschatka, but drank by way of infusion in brandy in Stotland.

———— AVIUM. *Common Wild Cherry-tree.* The fruit is black, and sometimes red, small, but sweet and agreeable to the taste, by fermentation making a grateful wine, and by distillation, bruised together with the stones, a strong spirit.

———— SPINOSA. *Black-thorn or Sloe-tree.* The bark of this shrub has been used by empirics to cure the ague. It will dye woollen of a red colour. The juice of it, with vitriol or copperas, will make good ink; and the fruit will make a very grateful and fragrant wine.

PYRUS MALUS. *Crab-apple.* This tree in its wild state is armed with prickles, and the fruit is extremely sour, and frequently bitter. Its juice, or *crab-vinegar*, applied outwardly, is good to cure spasms, cramps, strains, &c.

The bark will dye woollen of a citron colour.

It is remarkable for its longevity: it is said that some trees in Herefordshire have lived a thousand years.

The fruit, mixed with our cultivated apples, or even alone, if thoroughly ripe, will make a sound masculine cyder.

SPIRÆA FILIPENDULA. *Drop-wort.* The root consists of many tubercles, suspended by, and terminated with thread-like fibres. Swine are fond of the roots; and Linnæus informs us, that in a scarcity of corn they have been eaten by men instead of bread.

———— ULMARIA. *Meadow-sweet.* The whole plant is extremely fragrant: the common people in Sweden on holidays strew their floors with it.

A distilled water from the flowers has great efficacy in expelling the measles and small-pox. The whole plant has an astringent quality, and as such has been found useful in dysenteries, ruptures, and in tanning of leather. Horses and cows do not affect it, but goats are very fond of it.

ROSA CANINA. *Dog-rose.* The pulp of the fruit separated from the seeds, and mixed with wine and sugar, makes a jelly much esteemed in some countries. The bark with copperas dyes black.

RUBUS IDÆUS. *Raspberry-bush.* In the isle of Skye the juice or a syrup of the fruit is frequently used as an agreeable acid for making of punch, instead of oranges or lemons. A distilled water from the fruit is cooling, and very beneficial in fevers.

————— CASIUS. *Dewberry.* The fruit is blue when ripe, composed but of few *Acini,* and tasting like a mulberry.

————— FRUTICOSUS. *Common Bramble.* The leaves are astringent and drying ; a cataplasm made of them has been found serviceable in the erysipelas. The juice of the berries, fermented, will make a tolerably good wine.

————— SEXATILIS. *Stone Bramble.* The fruit is very acid alone, but eaten with sugar they make an agreeable dessert, and are esteemed antiscorbutic.

Russians ferment them with honey, and extract a potent spirit from them.

————— CHAMŒMORUS. *Cloudberries.* This plant is *diœcious* above ground, but, according to a curious observation made by Dr. Solander, the roots of the male and female unite together under the earth, so as to render the plant truly *monœcious.*

The berry is the size of a mulberry, when ripe of an orange colour, consisting of ten or twelve large acini, of a waterish or subacid taste.

The Swedes and Norwegians esteem the berries to be an excellent antiscorbutic : they preserve great quantities of them in the autumn to make tarts, and other confections. The Laplanders bruise and eat them as a delicious food in the milk of the rein deer ; and to preserve them through the winter, they bury them in snow, and at the return of spring find them as fresh and good as when first gathered.

In the highlands of Scotland we saw them produced at table as a dessert.

TORMENTILLA ERECTA. *Septfoil.* The roots consist of thick tubercles, an inch or more in diameter, replete with a red juice, of an astringent quality. They are used in most of the western isles, and in the Orknies, for tanning of leather ; in which intention they are proved, by some late experiments, to be superior even to the oak-bark. They are first of all boiled in water, and the leather afterwards steeped in the cold liquor. In the islands of Tirey and Col the inhabitants have destroyed so much ground by digging them up, that they have lately been prohibited the use of them.

A decoction of these roots in milk is also frequently administered by the inhabitants of the same islands in diarrhœas and dysenteries, with good success; but perhaps it would be most proper not to give it in dysenteries till the morbid matter be first evacuated. A spirituous extract of the plant stands recommended in the sea-scurvy, for to strengthen the gums and fasten the teeth. Linnæus informs us, that the Laplanders paint their leather of a red colour with the juice of the roots.

FRAGARIA vesca. *Wood Strawberry.* The root and leaves are astringent and vulnerary: the fruit will dissolve the tartar of the teeth, without acrimony: they have also a diuretic quality, and are found serviceable in the stone and gravel. Hoffman recommends them in fevers and consumptions, and Linnæus says, that by eating of them plentifully every day, when in season, he kept himself nearly free from the gout. A distilled water, or wine, as well as the fruit itself, may be used in cases of the stone, and a syrup in fevers.

GEUM urbanum. *Avens or Herb-Bennet.* The root is astringent: an infusion of it in wine, or thirty or forty grains of the powder, is esteemed a good medicine at the end of a dysentery.

———— rivale. *Red Water Avens.* It is found beneficial in diarrhœas and hœmorrhages, and in Canada we are told it is used instead of bark for agues.

POTENTILLA anserina. *Silver-weed.* It has an astringent quality, but is rarely used in medicine.

The roots taste like parsneps, and are frequently eaten by the common people in Scotland, either roast or boiled.

In the islands of Tirey and Col they are much esteemed, as answering in some measure the purposes of bread, they having been known to support the inhabitants for months together, during a scarcity of other provisions. They put a yoke on their ploughs, and often tear up their pasture grounds, with a view to eradicate the roots for their use; and as they abound most in barren and impoverished soils, and in seasons that succeed the worst for other crops, so they never fail to afford a most seasonable relief to the inhabitants in times of the greatest scarcity. A singular instance this of the bounty of Providence to these islands!

Cattle reject the leaves of this plant, but swine are fond of the roots.

COMARUM palustre. *Purple Marsh Cinquefoil.* The roots will dye wool of a red colour, and have astringency enough to tan leather.

After this account derived from the authorities of RAY, LINNÆUS, and LIGHTFOOT, which, if wished, might have been greatly extended,* no one need now ask *Cui Bono?* the study of Botany, in its extended sense, or even when limited to indigenous plants. In order to know these with precision, instead of relying on *traditionary accounts*, by means of *science* we arrive at the *names* of each unknown plant with an infallible certainty, and whilst in this pursuit we exercise both our reason and judgment. (Vide Preface, page viii.)

Every flower, however mean in the vulgar eye, is a sermon to the learned; and *indigenous plants*, as exhibiting themselves in every walk, merit certainly, although not always invested with the beauty of some *exotics*, the scrutinizing eye; for in their formation by the CREATOR OF THE UNIVERSE, will be found consummate wisdom and power. This pursuit produces in the mind an habit of order and arrangement (vide Preface, page vi), and it may be also observed that the bodily senses are highly improved by that accuracy and observation, which are necessary to discriminate the various objects that pass in review before them. This improvement may be carried to a degree, of which those who are inattentive to it have no idea. The *sight* of LINNÆUS was so penetrating, that he is said seldom or never to have used a glass, even in his minutest inquiries. But our own country affords a striking instance of an individual,† who, although wholly deprived of sight, has improved his other senses, his touch, his smell, and his taste, to such a degree, as to distinguish all the native plants of this country, with an accuracy not attained by many of those who have the advantages of sight, and which justly entitle him to rank with the first botanists of this kingdom.

---

* Vide our " *Medical Botany, or New Family Herbal,*" lately published, with wood-cuts of each plant by Bewick.

† Mr. Gough, of Kendal.

" Avoiding mankind," says the immortal *Rousseau*, " seeking solitude, no longer under the dominion of fancy, and indisposed towards
laborious reflection, possessing, nevertheless, a lively temperament,
which would not allow me to sink into a melancholy indifference, I
began to consider those objects of Nature which encompassed me,
and the choice fell to the study of Botany, for the following rea-
sons :—

" The *Mineral Kingdom* presented to me nothing in itself that was
lovely or attractive. Its riches, which are enclosed in the bowels of
the earth, seemed as if buried there, not to excite the avarice of
mankind. To profit from this study it demanded that I should be a
Chemist, and make the most painful and expensive experiments, work
in laboratories, expend much money and time, in coals, furnaces, cru-
cibles, retorts, amidst smoke, and *stifling* vapours, always at the *expense* of *health*, and oftentimes at the *hazard* of *life*.

" The *Animal Kingdom* is much more within our reach, and certainly merits our regard : nevertheless, has not this study its difficul-
ties, its embarrassments, its expenses, and its disgusts ? How are we
to observe, dissect, study, know, the birds flying in the air, the fishes
swimming in the waters, the quadrupeds avoiding our pursuits as swift
as the wind, or capable of resistance, and not more disposed to offer
themselves for my observations, than I to run after them, in order that
I might possess the pleasure of examining them ? Am I to pass a great
part of my life in being put out of breath by running after butterflies,
impaling of little insects which I may have entangled, and in the exa-
mination of snails and worms ? This study also requires a knowledge of *Anatomy*. By this alone we are enabled to class animals,
and distinguish the different genera. We must therefore study animals dead, dissect them, skeletonize them, and rake, at leisure, their
palpitating vitals. What a frightful apparatus is required for an
anatomical theatre ! It is not, upon my honour, in such a place that
Jean Jaque Rousseau will seek his instructions : and to study the
manners and dispositions of animals requires the game-keeper, the
fisherman, and fowler, and the expense of a vast menagerie, where
animals must undergo a deprivation of *liberty*, be confined in narrow
cages, and exhibit the frightful images of constraint, ennui, inquietude,
slavery, and torture, which no private advantages can justify.

" *Brilliant Flowers!* the enamel of the meadows: ye refreshing
shades, rivers, bowers, verdure! come purify my imagination, already

polluted by such an *hideous idea.* My soul, dead to all the great
movements in life, can only be affected by *innocent* scenes; from its
sensibility alone can be derived to it either pleasure or pain. . At-
tracted by *flowers,* which present themselves on every side, I observe,
I contemplate them, I compare them, in a word, I class them; and I
become so far a *Botanist* as one would wish, who studies Nature, so
as to derive from this pursuit an unceasing *satisfaction* or *contentment.*
To attain this knowledge I have no expensive works to purchase, nor
the trouble of diving into abstruse commentators; the book presented
me by Nature is quite sufficient, and without errata. I pass over it
with ease from herb to herb, from plant to plant, to compare their different characters, to remark their agreements and disagreements, in
short to examine their respective structures, to search into their laws,
the reason, and the end, of these animated machines—to give myself
up to the charms of unceasing admiration and gratitude towards that
BEING, who hath granted me all this indulgence.

" The *Botanist* at every walk pleasantly glides from object to object; each flower he examines excites in him curiosity and interest,
and as soon as he comprehends the manner of its structure, and the
rank it holds in a system, he enjoys an unalloyed pleasure, not less
vivid, because it costs him no great expense or trouble. In this oc-
cupation it is that the violent passions are lulled into a dead calm, and
only so much of emotion is produced as is sufficient to render life
happy and agreeable.

" All my *Botanical Excursions,*" continues *Rousseau,* " the several impressions which local objects gave, the ideas which in consequence sprung up, the little incidents which blended into the scene,
all these have produced a delightful impression, which the sight of my
herbarium at once rekindles. Although I may never again revisit
that beautiful country, those dark forests, those crystal lakes, those
hanging woods, those rugged rocks, those lofty mountains, whose sight
so often captivated my heart; although these happy scenes are closed
upon me for ever, yet am I transported back to them whenever I review the *herbarium* I possess. The little fragments of those plants I
collected are of themselves sufficient to recal the whole of this magni-
ficent spectacle. This *herbarium* of mine recommences for me a
journey of delight, and, as a camera obscura, repaints all this scenery
again to my view. It is this association which makes Botany so
charming; it recals back to the imagination all those ideas which af-

ford the truest pleasure. Meadows, water, woods, solitude, the *inward contentment*, which alone dwell among such objects, are incessantly brought forward to the memory. It at once transports me among inhabitants of peaceful beings, simple and kind, such as I should wish to pass my days with. It recals back my infant hours, my innocent pleasures, and compels me to forget every unhappiness."

It is thus that plants ever present themselves for our regards; they charm us by the beauty of their forms, the richness of their shades, and the pleasure they spread around our habitations; they alone afford delight, without leaving behind any inquietude. The heart overwhelmed with grief, the sight fatigued by exertion, find in the verdure of fields, adorned with flowers, both comfort and refreshment. Affecting spectacle! Thou calmest the anguish of the unfortunate, at the same time augmenting the happiness of those whose lot is prosperous! The waving CORN and golden sheaves delight every heart. We meet with other kindly VEGETABLES, which can assuage our pain and cure our maladies. I discover in vegetables the foundation of the *linen*, which I wear—of the *paper*, which hands down to us the wisdom of ages—those *dyes*, which impress on our garments their brilliant colours. To plants I am indebted for the *wood* which warms me in the winter, kindling into a blaze, resembling the sun I seem not now to want. Without *timber* my house could scarcely have been constructed; and when fashioned into *ships*, the world, which before was separated, with its produce, from me, by a vast expanse of waters, is now approached even to my very chamber. Hence I behold with still greater veneration those *trees*, whose stout branches diverge on every side, yet possessing a foliage which agreeably quivers to every breeze, but whose massy trunk shows an existence throughout ages.

Our Work *(a desideratum long required)* must be considered as an *Introduction* to the " FLORA BRITANNICA," by DOCTOR SMITH, and " ENGLISH BOTANY," where *all the Plants* of the *United Kingdom* have been *described* with *taste* and *judgment*, and *pourtrayed* with a fidelity that confers upon DOCTOR SMITH and Mr. SOWERBY an immortal honour!

CLASS I.... MONANDRIA.—ONE STAMEN.

DISCRIMINATING CHARACTERS

mparison.	2ᵈ Comparison.	3ʳᵈ Comparison.	4ᵗʰ Comparison.	5ᵗʰ Comparison.	6ᵗʰ Comparison.	GENERA and EXCEPTIONAL SPECIES.

MONANDRIA

The Pistilla in common circumstances.

Order I. MONOGYNIA. Flowers Bisexual simple.
- A Corolla .... 1. Valeriana rubra. Vide Class III. and plate 6. p. 6.
- No Corolla...
  - Stigma bifid......... 1. SALICORNIA. Vide Plate 11 page 11 (f).
  - Stigma acute......... 2. HIPPURIS ? Vide pl. 12. p. 12. (e)

Order II. DIGYNIA. (Bisexual simple)
- A Corolla (a)......... 3. CALLITRICHE. Vide pl. 13. p. 13. (a) (a)
- No Corolla .... 2. Aphanes Alchemilla. Vide Class IV. pl. 7. p. 7.

Order III. GYNANDRIA. (Bisexual complex)
- A Spadix
  - Spadix round......... 4. ARUM. Vide pl. 14. p. 14. (e)
  - Spadix flat......... 5. ZOSTERA. Vide pl. 15. p. 15. (a)
- No Spadix
  - A Corolla...
    - Flowers on one side only. } 3. Ophrys spiralis? Vide Class II. pl. 8. p. 8.
    - Flowers not so placed. } 4. Ophrys ovata. Vide Class II. pl. 9. p. 9.
  - No Corolla......... 5. Hippuris vulgaris. Vide Genus 2 above. pl. 10. p. 10.

The Pistilla peculiarly circumstanced.

Order IV. MONOECIA. (Unisexual)
- A Filament.
  - One Pistillum......... 6. Salix monandra. Vide Class II.
  - Two Pistilla......... 7. Callitriche aquatica Vide Genus 3 above. pl. 13. (d)
  - 4 or 5 Pistilla......... 6. ZANNICHELLIA. Vide pl. 16. p. 16. (e)
- No Filament.
  - A Spadix......... 8 Arum maculatum. Vide Genus 4 above.
  - No Spadix......... 7. CHARA. Vide pl. 17. p. 17.

Order V. POLYGAMIA. (Bis-uni-sexual)
- A Corolla......... 9. Callitriche aquatica Vide Genus 3 above.
- No Corolla......... 10. Hippuris vulgaris Vide Genus 2 above.

London Published for Dr. Thornton Jan 1. 1812.

Tab 2

CLASS II....DIANDRIA._TWO STAMINA.

DISCRIMINATING CHARACTERS.

GENERA and RECEPTIONAL SPECIES.

1st Comparison.	2nd Comparison.	3rd Comparison.	4th Comparison.	5th Comparison.	6th Comparison.	
		Tubular border flat.	Tube longer than the involucral Calyx.	. . . . . .		8. LIGÚSTRUM. Vide plate 22. page 22.
			Tube shorter than the involucral Calyx.			9. VERÓNICA. Vide pl. 23. p. 23.
	One-petalled.		Corolla spurred.	Calyx one leaved.		10. PINGUÍCULA. Vide pl. 24. p. 24.
				Calyx two leaved.		11. UTRICULÁRIA. Vide pl. 25. p. 25.
		Tubular, Border vergent.	Corolla not spurred.	The anther-bearing filaments fixed by the middle to two smaller filaments.		12. SÁLVIA. Vide pl. 26. p. 26.
				No such character.	Filaments curved.	13. VERBÉNA. Vide pl. 27. p. 27.
					Filaments straight.	14. LYCÓPUS. Vide pl. 28. p. 28.
1. MONOGYNIA.	Two-petalled.	. . . . . .				15. CIRCÉA. Vide pl. 29. p. 29.
	Four-petalled.	A Shido.				1. Fráxinus excélsior. Vide pl. 30. p. 30.
		A Capsule.				2. Corníspus dídyma. Vide Class IV.
			A Pericarp.	A Silicle.		3. Lepídium ruderále. Vide Class IV.
				A Capsule.		4. Fráxinus excélsior Vide Genus 26 below.
	A-petalled.	Calyx not a glume.	Pericarp, Calyx serving the office			5. Salicórnia herbácea. Vide Class II. Gen. 1.
		Calyx a glume.	Leaves prickly. Flower in corymbus.			6. Schœnus marísous Vide Class III.
			Leaves setaceous Flower farcicular.			7. Schœnus albus. Vide Class III.
2. DIGYNIA.	. . . . . .					16. ANTHÓXANTHUM. Vide pl. 31. p. 31.
	Nectary horn-shaped.					17. ÓRCHIS. Vide pl. 32. p. 32.
	bag-form.					18. SÁTYRIUM. Vide pl. 33. p. 33.
	slightly keeled.					19. ÓPHRYS. Vide pl. 34. p. 34.
3. GYNANDRIA.	ovate.					20. SERÁPIAS. Vide pl. 35. p. 35.
	inflated.					21. CYPRIPÉDIUM. Vide pl. 36. p. 36.
	erect.					22. MÁLAXIS. Vide pl. 37. p. 37.
4. MONŒCIA.						23. LÉMNA. Vide pl. 38. p. 38.
5. DIŒCIA. A Catkin.						24. SÁLIX. Vide pl. 39. p. 39.
6. POLYGÁMIA DIŒCIA. No Catkin. . . .						25. FRÁXINUS. Vide Genus 16 above.

London. Published for Dr. Thornton Jan.y 1.st 1812.

CLASS III....TRIANDRIA. THREE STAMINA.

				GENERA AND EXCEPTIONAL SPECIES.

DISCRIMINATING CHARACTERS.

4ᵗʰ Comparison. 5ᵗʰ Comparison. 6ᵗʰ Comparison. 7ᵗʰ Comparison.

Tab. I.
SIGMIA.

- Calyx not a glume:
  - Corolla, 5 parted . . . . **26. VALERIÁNA.**
  - Corolla, 6 parted:
    - Laciniæ all erect . . . . **27. CRÓCUS.**
    - Laciniæ, 3 reflexed, 3 erect . . . . . . **28. ÍRIS.**
- Calyx, a glume:
  - A Corolla . . . . **29. NÁRDUS.**
  - No Corolla:
    - Seeds encompassed with long wool . . . . **30. ERIÓPHORUS.**
    - Without such remarkable character:
      - Calyx-glumes crowded . . } **31. SCHŒNUS.**
      - partially imbricated } **32. CYPÉRUS.**
      - on every side imbricated } **33. SCÍRPUS.**

For **DYGYNIA**, and the other Orders, Vide Tab. 4. and 5.

London. Published for Dr. Thornton Jan. 1. 1812.

Tab. 4.

CLASS III. continued.

DISCRIMINATING CHARACTERS.

Comparisons.

GENERA
and
EXCEPTIONAL
SPECIES.

Calyx 3-valved . . . . 34 PANICUM.

Calyx involving one flower

Corolla 1 valve . . . . 35. ALOPECURUS.

2 valved

Calyx conspicuous for —
Valves truncated . . . . 36 PHLEUM.
— carinata . . . . 37. PHALARIS.
— ventricose . . . . 38. MILIUM.
— compressed . . . . 39. DACTYLIS.

2 valves

Corolla conspicuous by —
A feathery Arista . . . . 40. STIPA.
Exterior Valve, with 3 Aristas . . . . 41. LAGURUS.

Valves covered with much Wool —
leaves lanceolate . . . 1. Arundo epigeios. Vide Genus 49 below.
— linear . . . 2. Arundo calamagrosis.
— involute . . . 3. Arundo arenaria.

two flowers

both perfect —
scattered . . . . 42 AIRA
spiked . . . . 43. ELYMUS

one barren . . . . 4. Melica uniflora. Vide Genus 44.

many flowers

3 flowers, 1 barren . . . . 44. MELICA.

flowers scattered

Valves of Calyx, obtuse —
Spikelets cordate, distichous . . . . 45. BRIZA.
— oblong . . . . 46. POA.

many flowers

acute —
Corolla armed with Arista or wool —
Arista straight . . . 47. BROMUS.
— bristed . . . 48. AVENA.
Flosules woolly . . . 49. ARUNDO.

No arista or wool —
Stigma and style simple . . . . . . 50. FESTUCA.
— feathery . . . 5. Dactylis glomerata. Vide Genus 39.

spiked

Calyx 1 valve —
Corolla 1 valve . . . . 51. LOLIUM.
— 2 Valves . . . . 52. ROTTBOLLIA.

2 valves —
3 flowers, a long awn . . . . 53. HORDEUM.

Many flowered —
Involucre pinnatifid, or comb-shaped . . . . 54. CYNOSURUS.
No such character . . . . 55. TRITICUM.

London, Published for Dr. Thornton, Jany. 1st 1812.

Tab. 5.

CLASS III. continued.

DISCRIMINATING CHARACTERS.

Comparisons.

GENERA
and
EXCEPTIONAL
SPECIES.

Gr III GYNIA.
- Calyx 1 leaf .... 6. Tillæa muscosa. Vide Class IV.
- 2 leaves .... 56. MONTIA.
- 3 leaves
  - Petals emarginate, small .... 57. POLYCARPON.
  - 3 parted
    - Capsule opening at the apex .... 58. HOLOSTEUM.
    - 6 valves .... 7. Stellaria media. Vide Class X.

Gr IV. IŒCIA
- Calyx 1 leaf .... 59. BRYONIA.
- 3 or 5 leaves
  - A proper Calyx .... 60. AMARANTHUS.
  - An Ament
    - Ament globular .... 61. SPARGANIUM.
    - cylindrical
      - Perianth proper .... 62. TYPHA.
      - Calyx a scale .... 63. CAREX.
- glumes, 2 leaves
  - A round head .... Juncus conglomeratus. Vide Class VI.
  - A Panicle .... 9. Juncus effusus.

Gr V. IA.
- Calyx obscure .... 10. Valeriana dioica. Vide Class III.
- determinate
  - Calyx a scale
    - Plant Grass-like .... 11. Carex dioica. Vide Genus 63.
    - A Tree .... 12. Salix triandra. Vide Class II.
  - not a scale
    - A Perianth 3 parted .... 64. EMPETRUM.
    - 5 toothed .... 13. Bryonia dioica. Vide Genus 59.

Gr VII. ANDRIA.
- Calyx enclosing 2 flowers .... 65. HOLCUS.
- 3 flowers
  - Calyx Glumes 2, truncated .... 66. ÆGILOPS.
  - 6, not truncated
    - Involucre ciliate .... 14. Hordeum murinum. Vide Genus 53.
    - setaceous .... 15. Hordeum pratense.
    - neither ciliate or setaceous .... 16. Hordeum marinum.

London, Published for Dr Thornton. Jan 1. 1812.

Tab.6.

Clafs IV. TETRANDRIA. Four Stamina.

DISCRIMINATING CHARACTERS.

Genera & Exceptional Species.

Sections.

1. Flowers, 1-petalled,1-seeded, superior (aggregate)
- Proper Calyx, double................... 67 Scabiosa.
- ———— single.......................... 68 Dipsacus.

II. ——— 2-seeded, superior (stellatæ)
- Corol. bell-shaped...................... 69 Rúbia.
- ——— rotate............................ 70 Galium.
- ——— funnel-shaped
  - Seed, crownlefs...................... 71 Aspérula.
  - ——— crowned........................ 72 Sherardia.

Order I. Monogynia. III. ——— many seeded, inferior.
- Tubulous
  - Tube, free
    - Tube ventricose. (Corol. salver-shaped).. 73 Exacum.
  - Throat, naked ——— strait
    - Border 4-cleft reflext, Stam. long.... 74 Plantago.
    - ——— spreading, Stam. short......... 75 Centúnculus.
  - Tube, closed with hairs................

IV. ——— 1-seeded, superior (flowers not of the natural order the aggregatæ.) 76 Sanguisorba.

V. 4-petalled. many-seeded, inferior.
- A Silique
  - separating in the ordinary course....... 77 Epimédium.
  - becoming revolute....... 1 Cardamine hirsuta, Vide a.n.
- A Silicle....... 2 Coronopus didyma, Vide a.n.

VI. ——— superior (a Tree) .... 78 Cornus.

——— apetalled .... 79 Alchemilla.

Order II. Digynia.
- Corolla 4-petalled............ 80 Buffonia.
- 1-petalled
  - Plant not parasitical........... 3 Gentiana campestris, Vide a.n.
  - ——— parasitical.............. 4 Cuscuta Europæa, Vide a.n.

Order III. Tetragynia.
- 1-petalled................... 81 Ilex.
- 4-petalled
  - Calyx 3, 4, & 5-cleft (Capsules 3 to 5.)...... 82 Tillǽa.
  - ——— none. (Seeds 4-naked.)........... 83 Potamógeton.
  - ——— many-cleft (Capsules 8-celled, 8-valved.).. 84 Radíola.
  - ——— 4-leaved (Capsule 1-celled.)......... 85 Sagína.
  - ——— 5-leaved (Petals bifid.)..... 5 Cerástium tetrandrum Vide a.n.

Order Didynamia * for which Vide Tab. 7.
- Neither Calyx, or Corolla............. 86 Rúppia.

Order IV. Monoecia.
- Trees or Shrubs
  - A Corolla
    - 1-Petalled (4-parted.)............ 87 Betula.
    - 2-Petalled................... 88 Búxus.
  - No Corolla............. 6 Myrica Gale, Vide Gen.
- Herbs
  - A Corolla
    - Monopetalous, 2-parted.......... 89 Eriocáulon.
    - ——— 4-cleft.............. 90 Littorélla.
  - No Corolla (Calyx 4-leaved.).......... 91 Urtíca.

Order V. Dioecia.
- Trees or Shrubs
  - Calyx an Ament............ 92 Mýrica.
  - ——— not an Ament....... 7 Rhámnus cathárticus, Vide a.n.
- Herbs
  - No Corolla
    - Calyx 2-Parted............ 93 Hippóphae.
    - ——— 4-D?........... 8 Urtica Dioica, Vide Gen. &c.
  - A Corolla. (Petals 4.)........... 94 Viscum.

Order VI. Polygamia.
- No Calyx................. 95 Valántia.
- A Calyx (4-Cleft.)........... 96 Parietária.

* For Order VII. Didynamia, 4 Stamina, 2 long & 2 short; flowers Ringent or Personate. Vide Tab. 7. It might have constituted Order IV. but for the convenience of the Tabular form is made as the concluding Order.—

Tab. I.

Class IV. TETRANDRIA, concluded.

DISCRIMINATING CHARACTERS.

Didynamia.

Sect. 1. Four naked Seeds imbedded in the Calyx.

Genera & Exceptional Species.

Anthers, sprinkled with Osseous points.	97 Leonúrus
_____. each pair forming a crofs.	98 Glecóma
_____. crofsed (Corolla, upper lip flat.)	99 Melittis
Filaments forked at their apices.	100 Prunélla
Stamina, having performed their office, turned to the sides} (Lower lip reflected at the sides)	101 Stáchis
Filaments, distant, strait.	102 Méntha
Calyx, when in fruit covered with a lid.	103 Scutellária
_____. throat, closed with hairs.	104 Thymus
An Involucre, or Strobile collecting the Calyxes.	105 Origanum
_____ narrow-leaved, or many-bristled, collecting the Calyxes.	106 Clinopódium
Calyx, having one Tooth truncated. (Subringent.)	9 Verbena officinális Vide Cl. I.
_____ cleft, having ten Striæ.{upper lip of the Corolla arched.	107 Ballóta
{strait, two-cleft.	108 Marrúbium
Upper lip, two-parted beyond the base.	109 Teucrium
_____. very small.	110 Ajugá
_____. flat, ascending, tube cylindrical.	111 Betónica
Under lip, with 2 teeth above.	112 Galeópsis
_____. 3-cleft, segments acute.	113 Galeóbdolon
_____. crenate; throat with the margin reflexed.	114 Népeta
Throat, toothed on each side.	115 Lámium

Sect. 2. Several Seeds fixed in a Receptacle in the middle of a Pericarp.

Corolla ringent; Leaflets of the Calyx, lateral, lobed; Capsule 1-celled.	116 Orobánche
Remarkable in the Anthers, being 2-lobed, & the under ending in a thorn} Capsule 2-celled; Seeds striated}	117 Euphrásia
_____ in having an inflated Calyx; Capsule 2-celled; Seeds com-} prefsed, flat, imbricated.}	118 Rhinánthus
_____ in having a gland under the germen; the upper lip ending} in a harrow hook; Capsule 1-celled}	119 Lathróea
_____ in the Calyx being colored above, sublabiate, teeth obtuse; cap-} sule 2-celld; seeds angular, marked with 2 eminences in the middle; seeds 2, gibbous, shining.}	120 Bártsia
Corolla quite closed in some species, but the lateral margins are reflexed. lower lip as long as the upper, half 3-cleft; segments equal}	121 Melampýrum

N.B. In the above the Corollas are all Ringent.

Remarkable in the Corolla's being rotate, Capsule 2-celld, difsepiment transverse.	122 Sibthórpia
_____ companulate, Calyx above the germen; fruit a} berry, dry, 3-cell'd.}	123 Linnóea
_____ beneath the germen; a Capsule, imperfectly 2-cell'd.	124 Limosélla
_____ Subringent, tube ventricose; Capsule 2-celled.	125 Digitális
_____ Ringent reversed, instead of the Stamina arising} from above, affixed to the under lip which seems formed as the upper; Capsule 2-cell'd}	126 Scrophulária
_____ Personatr. {Nectary a spur, Capsule 2-celled.	127 Antirrhínum
{No Nectary, helmet comprefsed, Capsule 2-celld, seeds mucronate.	128 Pediculáris

London, Publifhed by Dr. Thornton, 1812.

Tab 8.

Clafs V. PENTANDRIA. Five Stamina.

DISCRIMINATING CHARACTERS.

Genera

					Genera
Order 1. mogynia. Section 1. ...l. 1-petalled: ...id Seeds. ...ers rough.	Throat naked	Corol. bell-shaped			129 Echium
		funnel-shap'd	Calyx 5 seeded		130 Pulmonária
			No such character		131 Lithospérmum
	arch(d)	Corol. funnel-shap'd	Tube, strait	Anthers, conceal'd: Tube, prismatic at the base	132 Anchúsa
				No such character	133 Aspérugo
			exposed		134 Cynoglófsum
		curved			135 Lycópsis
		wheel-shaped			136 Myosótis
	toothed	rotate			137 Borágo
		bell-shaped			138 Sýmphytum

Sect 2. rol. 1-petalld. ...s enclosed. ...s smooth. ...m superior.	Corol. rotate	A Capsule	1 celled	Capfule, dividing in the middle into 2 valves	139 Anagállis
				splitting into 10 valves	140 Lysimáchia
				without determination of valves	141 Hottónia
			2	Anthers, spirally twisted	142 Chirónia
				No such character	143 Verbáscum
			3		144 Polemónium
		Berry	Covered by a Capsule		145 Cýclamen
			No such character, Berry 2-celled		146 Solánum
		Follicle			147 Vínca
	bell-shap'd	1-Stigma	Stamens inserted into the Receptacle		148 Azálea
			base of the Corolla		149 Átropa
		2-Stigmata			150 Convólvulus
	funnel-shap'd	Having a fringed Corolla			151 Menyánthes
		No such character	Capsule 1-celled mouth 10-cleft		152 Prímula
			2 celled	Capsule having a lid over it	153 Hyoscýamus
				No such character, 1-valved	154 Datúra

Sect 3. ...as Sect 2. ...m inferior.	Corolla bell-shaped			155 Campánula
	salver-shaped			156 Samolús
	rotate			157 Phyteúma
	subringent			158 Lonicéra
Sect 4. 5-petalled. ...m superior.	Calyx urceolate, fruit a berry			159 Rhámnus
	flat, fruit a Capsule			160 Euonymus
Sect 5 petalled. inferior.	Style simple			161 Hederá
	4 cleft			162 Ríbes
Sect 6. apetalled.	Calyx 1-leaved	colored, not stameniferous		163 Gláux
		not colored, stameniferous		164 Thésium
	5 leaved			165 Illecébrum

NB. For Orders 2. Digynia, 3. Trigynia, 4. Tetragynia, 5. Pentagynia, 6. Hexagynia, 7. Monœcia, 8. Diœcia, 9. Polygamia, 10. Syngenesia, & 11. Monogamia, Vide Tab. 9. 10. 11. 12. 13. & 14.

London, Published by Dr. Thornton, 1812.

DISCRIMINATING CHARACTERS.

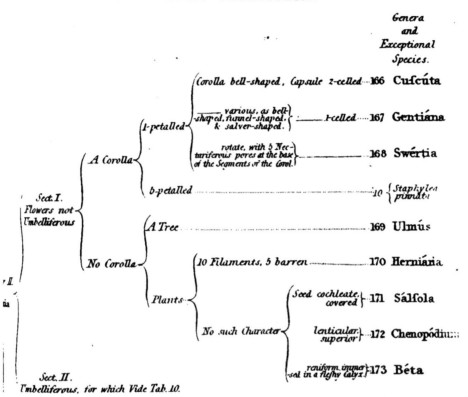

Genera
and
Exceptional
Species.

Corolla bell-shaped, Capsule 2-celled···· 166 **Cufcúta**

——— various, as bell-shaped, funnel-shaped, & salver-shaped. } ——— 1-celled ···· 167 **Gentiána**

rotate, with 5 Nec-tariferous pores at the base of the Segments of the Corol. } ——————— 168 **Swértia**

5-petalled ·· 10 { *Staphylea pinnata*

A Tree ·· 169 **Ulmús**

10 Filaments, 5 barren ———————— 170 **Herniária**

Seed cochleate, covered } 171 **Sálfola**

lenticular, superior } 172 **Chenopódium**

reniform, immer-sal in a fleshy Calyx } 173 **Béta**

1-petalled

A Corolla

5-petalled

No Corolla

Plants

No such Character

Sect. I.
Flowers not Umbelliferous

Sect. II.
Umbelliferous, for which Vide Tab. 10.

London, Publifhed by Dʳ Thornton, Janʸ 1, 1812.

Clafs V. PENTANDRIA, continued.

DISCRIMINATING CHARACTERS.

Sect. I. Umbels simple.

Genera &
Exceptional Species.

		Character	Genus
		Scarce any umbel (5 flowers only; involucre 4-leaved; petals entire; seeds orbicular, compressed)	174 Hydrocótyle.
		Umbel, capitate, (floscules seffile; involucre many-leaved; receptacle common, conical chaffy; seeds muricated)	175 Erýngium.
		—— subcapitate, (floscules seffile; petals inflexed; flowers of the difk. abortive: seeds muricated with hooked setæ)	176 Sanicula.

Involucre

Sect. II. True umbelliferous flowers; universal umbel composed of few rays.

General.	Partial.	Character	Genus
Sect. I. Heared	1 to 3-leaved	Involucells halved: Fruit spherical.	177 Coriándrum.
1 or 4-leaved	4-leaved	Petals inflexed: Seeds ovate striated.	178 Sison.
few-leaved	5-leaved	Involucre simple: Seeds muricated.	179 Caúcalis.
Sect. II. many-leaved	——	Petals involute: Seeds compressed striated.	180 Buplerum.
——	many-leaved	Corolla difform, radiate, florets of the ray abortive: Seed crowned, seffile suberose corticated.	181 Œnanthe.
——	——	—— uniform, florets all of them fertile: Petals cordate. Seeds nearly ovate, striated.	182 Sium.

Sect. III. Universal Umbel composed of many rays.

General.	Partial.	Character	Genus
Sect. I. 2-leaved	Heared, 6-cleft, thorny	Flowers radiate, abortive, central ones female: Seed immersed in the involucret.	183 Echinóphora.
setaceous	4 or 5-leaves, dimidiate, setaceous, & scabrous	—— —— fertile: Seed crenate at the margin.	184 Tordýlium.
——	8-leaved	—— flosculous, fertile: Petals incurved, umbellets round: Seeds hemispherical, 3-winged.	185 Angélica.
——	many-leaved, pinnatifid, incised	—— —— —— inflexed: Seed elliptic-oblong with 3-prominences on each side.	186 Meum.
3 cleft, membranous	many leaved, entire	—— —— —— involute entire: Seed oblong with 3-prominences, scarcely visible.	187 Ligústicum.
Sect. II. many leaved, leaves pinnatifid	1-leaved, simple or 3-cleft	—— radiate, abortive: Seed muricated.	188 Daucus.
——	3 or 4-leaved, dimidiate or halved	—— flosculous, fertile: Petals cordate: Seed gibbous ribb'd & furrow'd.	189 Cónium.
——	3 to 7-leaved, exterior longest	—— radiate, abortive: Involucre deciduous: Seed membranous, compressed.	190 Herácleum.
very short simple	many-leaved	—— incurved: Flowers flosculous, abortive: Seed compressed striated in the middle.	191 Peucédanum.
——	——	—— inflexed cordate, —— —— fertile: Seed convex, striated.	192 Alhamánta.
margin membranous	——	—— cordate, —— —— —— Seed compressed, striated in the middle.	193 Selínum.
——	setaceous	—— —— —— —— Seed ovate.	194 Búnium.
——	——	—— inflexed: —— —— —— Seed oval, compressed, striated.	195 Crithmum.

For Sect. II. No Universal, but only a Partial Involucre, & Sect. III. No Universal or Partial Involucre, Vide Tab. II.

Davies fc.

London, Publifhed by Dr. Thornton, 1812.

Clafs V. PENTANDRIA, continued.

DISCRIMINATING CHARACTERS.

Sect. I. Umbels simple.

			Genera & Exceptional Species
	Some any umbel (5 flowers only; involucre 4-leaved; petals entire; seeds orbicular, compressed)		174 Hydrocótyle.
	Umbel, capitate, (floscules sessile; involucre many-leaved; receptacle common, conical chaffy; Seeds muricated.)		175 Eryngium.
	—— subcapitate, (floscules sessile; petals inflexed; flowers of the disk, abortive; seeds muricated with hooked setæ.)		176 Sanicula.

Involucre

Sect. II. True umbelliferous flowers; universal umbel composed of few rays.

General.	Partial.		Genera & Exceptional Species
Sect. I. 1-leaved	1 to 3-leaved	Involucells halved: Fruit spherical.	177 Coriándrum.
1 or 4-leaved	4-leaved	Petals inflexed: Seeds ovate striated.	178 Sison.
1 or-leaved	5-leaved	Involucre simple: Seeds muricated.	179 Caúcalis.
Sect. II. many-leaved	——	Petals involute: Seeds compressed striated.	180 Bupleurum.
——	many-leaved	Corolla difform, radiate, florets of the ray abortive: Seed crowned, sessile suberose corticated.	181 Œnanthe.
——	——	—— uniform, florets all of them fertile: Petals cordate. Seeds nearly ovate, striated.	182 Sium.

Sect. III. Universal Umbel composed of many rays.

General.	Partial.		Genera & Exceptional Species
Sect. I. 1-leaved	1-leaved, 6-cleft thorny	Flowers radiate, abortive, central ones female: Seed immersed in the involucret.	183 Echinóphora.
setaceous	4 or 5-leaves, dimidiate, setaceous, & scabrous	—— —— fertile: Seed crenate at the margin.	184 Tordýlium.
——	8-leaved	—— flosculous, fertile: Petals incurved, umbellets round: Seeds hemispherical, 3-winged.	185 Angélica.
——	many-leaved, pinnatifid, incised	—— —— —— inflexed: Seed elliptic-oblong with 3 prominences on each side.	186 Meum.
3 cleft, membranous	many leaved, entire	—— —— —— involute entire: Seed oblong with 3 prominences, scarcely visible.	187 Ligústicum.
Sect. II. many leaved, lower pinnatifid	1-leaved, simple or 3-cleft	—— radiate, abortive: Seed muricated.	188 Daucus.
——	3 or 4-leaved, dimidiate, or halved	—— flosculous, fertile: Petals cordate. Seed gibbous ribbed & furrowed.	189 Cónium.
——	3 to 7-leaved, exterior longest	—— radiate, abortive: Involucre deciduous: Seed membranous, compressed.	190 Herácleum.
ray short simple	many-leaved	incurved: Flowers flosculous, abortive: Seed compressed striated in the middle.	191 Peucédanum.
——	——	inflexed cordate, —— —— fertile: Seed convex, striated.	192 Alhamánta.
margin membranous	——	cordate, —— —— —— : Seed compressed, striated in the middle.	193 Selinum.
——	setaceous	—— —— —— , —— : Seed ovate.	194 Búnium.
——	——	inflexed : —— —— —— : Seed oval, compressed, striated.	195 Crithmum.

For Sect. II. No Universal, but only a Partial Involucre, & Sect. III. No Universal or Partial Involucre. Vide Tab. II.

Davies ft.

London, Published by Dr. Thornton, 1812.

Clafs V. PENTANDRIA, continued.

DISCRIMINATING CHARACTERS.

			Genera & Exceptional Species.

Sect. I. Umbels simple.

	Genera & Exceptional Species.
Some any umbel (5 flowers only; involucre 4-leaved; petals entire; seeds orbicular, compressed)	174 Hydrocótyle.
Umbel, capitate, (floscules sessile; involucre many-leaved; receptacle common, conical chaffy; Seeds muricated.)	175 Erýngium.
—— subcapitate, (flosculos sessile; petals inflexed; flowers of the disk, abortive; seeds muricated with hooked seta.)	176 Sanícula.

Involucre

General.	Partial.	Sect. II. True umbelliferous flowers; universal umbel composed of few rays.	
Sect. I. Heared	1 to 3-leaved	Involucells halved: Fruit spherical.	177 Coriándrum.
3 or 4-leaved	4-leaved	Petals inflexed: Seeds ovate striated.	178 Sison.
few-leaved	5-leaved	Involucre simple: Seeds muricated.	179 Caúcalis.
Sect. II. many-leaved	——	Petals involute: Seeds compressed striated.	180 Bupleurum.
——	many-leaved	Corolla difform, radiate, florets of the ray abortive: Seed crowned, sessile suberose corticated.	181 Œnanthe.
	——	—— uniform, florets all of them fertile: Petals cordate. Seeds nearly ovate, striated.	182 Sium.

		Sect. III. Universal Umbel composed of many rays.	
Sect. I. 3-leaved	Heared, 6-cleft thorny	Flowers radiate, abortive, central ones female: Seed immersed in the involucret.	183 Echinóphora.
setaceous	4 or 5-leaves, dimidiate, setaceous, & scabrous	—— —— fertile: Seed crenate at the margin.	184 Tordýlium.
——	8-leaved	—— flosculous, fertile: Petals incurved, umbellets round: Seeds hemispherical, 3-winged.	185 Angélica.
——	many-leaved, pinnatifid, incised	—— —— —— inflexed: Seed elliptic-oblong with 3-prominences on each side.	186 Meum.
3 cleft, membranous	many leaved, entire	—— —— —— involute entire: Seed oblong with 3-prominences, scarcely visible.	187 Ligústicum.
Sect. II. many leaved, leaves pinnatifid	3-leaved, simple or 3-cleft	—— radiate, abortive: Seed muricated.	188 Daucus.
——	3 or 4-leaved, dimidiate or halved	—— flosculous, fertile: Petals cordate: Seed gibbous ribbed & furrowed.	189 Cónium.
——	3 to 7-leaved, exterior longest	—— radiate, abortive: Involucre deciduous: Seed membranous, compressed.	190 Herácleum.
very short simple	many-leaved	incurved: Flowers flosculous, abortive: Seed compressed striated in the middle.	191 Peucédanum.
——	——	inflexed cordate, —— —— fertile: Seed convex, striated.	192 Alhamánta.
margin membranous	——	cordate: —— —— —— : Seed compressed, striated in the middle.	193 Selínum.
——	setaceous	—— —— —— : Seed ovate.	194 Búnium.
——	——	inflexed: —— —— —— : Seed oval, compressed, striated.	195 Crithmum.

For Sect. II. No Universal, but only a Partial Involucre, & Sect. III. No Universal or Partial Involucre, Vide Tab. II.

Davies ft.

London, Publihed by Dr Thornton, 1812.

Clafs V. PENTANDRIA, continued.

DISCRIMINATING CHARACTERS.

Sect. I. Umbels simple.

	Genera & Exceptional Species.
Some any umbel (5 flowers only; involucre 4-leaved; petals entire; seeds orbicular, compressed)	174 Hydrocótyle.
Umbel, capitate, (floscules sessile; involucre many-leaved; receptacle common, conical chaffy; Seeds muricated)	175 Eryngium.
—— subcapitate, (flosculos sessile; petals inflexed; flowers of the disk abortive; seeds muricated with hooked setæ)	176 Sanicula.

Involucre

General. Sect. I.	Partial.	Sect. II. True umbelliferous flowers; universal umbel composed of few rays.	Genera & Exceptional Species.
3-leaved	1 to 3-leaved	Involucells halved: Fruit spherical.	177 Coriándrum.
3 or 4-leaved	4-leaved	Petals inflexed: Seeds ovate striated.	178 Sison.
few-leaved	5-leaved	Involucre simple: Seeds muricated.	179 Caúcalis.
Sect. II. many-leaved	——	Petals involute: Seeds compressed striated.	180 Buplcurum.
——	many-leaved	Corolla difform, radiate, florets of the ray abortive: Seed crowned, sessile suberose corticated.	181 Œnanthe.
——	——	—— uniform, florets all of them fertile: Petals cordate. Seeds nearly ovate, striated.	182 Sium.

		Sect. III. Universal Umbel composed of many rays.	
Sect. I. 2-leaved	3-leaved, 6-cleft thorny	Flowers radiate, abortive, central ones female: Seed immersed in the involucret.	183 Echinóphora.
setaceous	4 or 5-leaves, dimidiate, setaceous, & scabrous	—— —— fertile: Seed crenate at the margin.	184 Tordýlium.
——	8-leaved	—— flosculous, fertile: Petals incurved, umbellets round: Seeds hemispherical, 3-winged.	185 Angélica.
——	many-leaved, pinnatifid, incised	—— —— —— inflexed: Seed elliptic-oblong with 3-prominences on each side.	186 Meum.
3 cleft, membranous	many leaved, entire	—— —— —— involute entire: Seed oblong with 3-prominences, scarcely visible.	187 Ligústicum.
Sect. II. many leaved, lower pinnatifid	1-leaved, simple or 3-cleft	—— radiate, abortive: Seed muricated.	188 Daucus.
——	3 or 4-leaved, dimidiate or halved	—— flosculous, fertile: Petals cordate: Seed gibbous ribb'd & furrow'd.	189 Cónium.
——	3 to 7-leaved, exterior longest	—— radiate, abortive: Involucre deciduous: Seed membranous, compressed.	190 Heráclcum.
ray short simple	many-leaved	incurved: Flowers flosculous, abortive: Seed compressed striated in the middle.	191 Peucédanum.
——	——	inflexed cordate; —— —— fertile: Seed convex, striated.	192 Alhamánta.
margin membranous	——	cordate; —— ——, —: Seed compressed, striated in the middle.	193 Selínum.
——	setaceous	—— ——, —: Seed ovate.	194 Búnium.
——	——	inflexed: —— ——, —: Seed oval, compressed, striated.	195 Crithmum.

For Sect. II. No Universal, but only a Partial Involucre, & Sect. III. No Universal or Partial Involucre, Vide Tab. II.

Davies ft.

London, Published by Dr. Thornton, 1812.

Clafs V. PENTANDRIA, continued.

DISCRIMINATING CHARACTERS.

Sect. I. Umbels simple.

Character	Genera & Exceptional Species.
Scarce any umbel (5 flowers only; involucre 4-leaved; petals entire; seeds orbicular, compressed)	174 Hydrocótyle.
Umbel, capitate (floscules sessile; involucre many-leaved; receptacle common, conical chaffy; seeds muricated)	175 Eryngium.
——— subcapitate (floscules sessile; petals inflexed; flowers of the disk abortive; seeds muricated with hooked setæ)	176 Sanicula.

Involucre

Sect. II. True umbelliferous flowers; universal umbel composed of few rays.

General. Sect. I.	Partial.		Genera.
1-leaved	1 to 3-leaved	Involucells halved: Fruit spherical.	177 Coriándrum.
2 or 4-leaved	4-leaved	Petals inflexed: Seeds ovate striated.	178 Sison.
few-leaved	5-leaved	Involucre simple: Seeds muricated.	179 Caúcalis.
Sect. II. many-leaved	———	Petals involute: Seeds compressed striated.	180 Bupleurum.
———	many-leaved	Corolla difform, radiate, florets of the ray abortive: Seed crowned, sessile suberose corticated.	181 Œnanthe.
———	———	uniform, florets all of them fertile: Petals cordate. Seeds nearly ovate, striated.	182 Sium.

Sect. III. Universal Umbel composed of many rays.

General. Sect. I.	Partial.		Genera.
2-leaved	1-leaved, 6-cleft thorny	Flowers radiate, abortive, central ones female: Seed immersed in the involucret.	183 Echinóphora.
setaceous	4 or 5-leaves, dimidiate, setaceous, & scabrous	——— ——— fertile: Seed crenate at the margin.	184 Tordýlium.
———	8-leaved	——— flosculous, fertile: Petals incurved: umbellets round: Seeds hemispherical, 3-winged.	185 Angélica.
———	many-leaved, pinnatifid, incised	——— ——— ——— inflexed: Seed elliptic-oblong with 3-prominences on each side.	186 Meum.
3 cleft, membranous	many leaved, entire	——— ——— ——— involute entire: Seed oblong with 3-prominences, scarcely visible.	187 Ligústicum.
Sect. II. many leaved, leaves pinnatifid	1-leaved, simple or 3-cleft	——— radiate, abortive: Seed muricated.	188 Daucus.
———	3 or 4-leaved, dimidiate or halved	——— flosculous, fertile: Petals cordate: Seed gibbous ribb'd & furrow'd.	189 Cónium.
———	3 to 7-leaved, exterior longest	——— radiate, abortive: Involucre deciduous: Seed membranous, compressed.	190 Herácleum.
ray short simple	many-leaved	incurved: Flowers flosculous, abortive: Seed compressed striated in the middle.	191 Peucédanum.
———	———	inflexed cordate: ——— ——— fertile: Seed convex, striated.	192 Alhamánta.
margin membranous	———	cordate: ——— ———, ——— Seed compressed, striated in the middle.	193 Selínum.
———	setaceous	——— ———, ——— Seed ovate.	194 Búnium.
———	———	inflexed: ——— ———, ——— Seed oval, compressed, striated.	195 Crithmum.

For Sect. II. No Universal, but only a Partial Involucre, & Sect. III. No Universal or Partial Involucre, Vide Tab. II.

Davies ft.

London, Published by Dr. Thornton, 1812.

Clafs V. PENTANDRIA. continued.

DISCRIMINATING CHARACTERS.

Partial Involucre.

Genera.

Sect. I.
1 or 2 leaves setaceous ..... Florets flosculous, and fertile. Umbel expanding flat. Seed compressed surrounded by a margin — 196 Imperatória

3-leaves ..... Florets somewhat radiate, fertile. Involucells dimidiate, pendulous. Seed striated — 197 Æthúsa

5-leaves ..... Florets somewhat radiate; abortive involucells, reflexed, concave. Seed oblong, smooth — 198 Chærophýllum

Florets radiate, abortive; Seed subulate. ..... 199 Scandix

Sect. II.
many-leaves setaceous ..... Florets flosculous, fertile; Seed crowned ..... 200 Phellándrium

Florets flosculous, fertile; Seed nearly ovate, furrowed ..... 201 Cicúta

Note. Here we might have inserted Exceptional Species. 1. Bupleurum rotundifolium. 2. Caucalis infesta. 3. Angelica sylvestris. 4. Sium nodiflorum 5. Œnanthe fistulosa. 6. Peucedanifolia, which are often found wanting the general involucre, but as this part is very apt to vary, and the Seeds have been all discriminated in each Genus, which are lefs subject to variety, we shall omit these Exceptional Species. In the next section we are obligated to have recourse entirely to the Seeds, and in these difficult discriminations have given as many sources of comparison as can be required.

Florets.

Sect. I.
Seeds
Flosculous fertile, Petals inflexed — ribbed (Sometimes a one leaved involucre appears)...... 202 Apium

Stigma nearly globular, striated ..... 203 Pimpinélla

ovate, striated ..... 204 Egopódium

Stigma simple — Somewhat comprefsed 3 ribbed on each side ..... 205 Anéthum

comprefsed, flat ..... 206 Pastináca

Sect. II.
Flosculous abortive — reniform angular ..... 207 Smýrnium

gibbous, striated ..... 208 Cárum

Davies fc.

London, Publifhed by Dr. Thornton, Janr. 1. 1812.

Tab. 12.

Clafs V. PENTANDRIA, continued.

DISCRIMINATING CHARACTERS.

Genera
and
Exceptional Species.

Flowers difposed in a (yme, much refembling an umbel (Flowers fuperior) Berry 3-seeded	209 Sambucus
1-seeded	210 Viburnum
Order III. gynia not so difposed (inferior) Petals bipartite	11 Stellaria Média Vide Clafs X.
entire Capsules 3, connate, inflated	211 Staphilea
No such character Leaves of the Calyx, length of the Corol	212 Corrigiola
one half shorter than the Corol	213 Tamarix
Order IV. gynia Nectary ciliate with bristles, each terminated by a globule	214 Parnassia
Order V. agynia Calyx 1-leaved entire, scariose, flowers aggregate	215 Statice
10-cleft	216 Sibbaldia
5-leaved erect	217 Linum
spreading Petals bifid	12 Ceràstium semidecandrum Vide Cl. X.
entire	13 Spérgula arvensis pentandra & subulata
Order VI. gynia Leaves armed with points, which secrete each a globule of fluid, entangling flies	218 Drosera
Order VII. gynia Receptacle subulate, covered with numerous naked seeds	219 Myosurus
flat, bearing seeds capsuled	Ranunculus hederaceus Vide Cl. XII.
Order VIII. delphia Capsule 5-celled, each containing a single seed, or 5 naked seeds, arilled	Geranium cicutarium Moschatum Maritimum & Pimpinellifolium Vide Clafs X.

Heritier has improperly put these as a new Genus called them Erodium

*Order Syngenesia, might have come in here with more propriety, but not to have too many tables we have placed it as the last order in this Clafs.

Order IX. monœcia Male flowers Calyx common, imbricated	220 Xanthium
3-leaved	221 Amaranthus
5-toothed	222 Bryonia
5-parted	Atriplex Portulacoïdes Vide Gen. 224.
Female flowers Trees 4-cleft	Fagus sylvática Vide Cl. III.
very entire	Quercus robur Vide Cl. III.
Order X. Diœcia Calyx 5-leaved, Male flower 3-leaved, Female D?	223 Humulus
Order XI. ... gamia Calyx 1-parted, Male Flower 2-leaved, Females D?	224 Atriplex

*This comes into Tab. 13 as Order XI.

London, Publifhed by D? Thornton. 1812.

End of Col. 2

DISCRIMINATING CHARACTERS.

Section I. All the Florets Ligulate. (Polygamia æqualis of Linnæus, flowers bisexual.)

Forms of Calyx.	Scales.	Receptacle.	Pappus.	Genera
Sect. I. Imbricated Scales lax.	Flaccid Inner, linear Outer, reflexed.	Naked and deeply punctated.	Sect. I. Stipitate, simple covered by the Calyx which appears straight.	225 Leóntodon
(Ventricose) at the base.	very numerous, linear, unequal.	Naked & punctated.	Sect. II. Sessile simple covered by the Calyx converging into a depressed acuminate globe.	226 Sónchus
(Cylindrical)	very numerous, acuminate, membranous at the margins.		Stipitate, simple Calyx converging in an ovate-cylindrical form.	227 Lactúca
Ovate.	Several, linear, very unequal, longitudinal, and incumbent.	— — — —	Sessile, simple Calyx, converging ovate.	228 Hierácium
Roundish.	Lanceolate, ending acute.	Chaffy.	Plumose, Calyx converging Globular-acuminate.	229 Hypochéris
Sect. II. Calyculate Cylindrical.	8, narrow, lanceolate, 5, incumbent, shorter.	Somewhat Chaffy.	Chaffy Calyx cylindrical converging at the summit.	230 Cichórium
Ovate, angular.	of the tube, 8. ___ base, 6	Naked.	various or none Calyx scales embracing the nearest contiguous seeds.	231 Lapsána
Cylindrical smooth.	of the tube as many as Florets ___ base, few, unequal, short. Inner oval.	— — — —	hairy Calyx cylindrical slightly converging at the mouth.	232 Prenánthes
Sect. III. Double.	Inner, ovate, converging Outer, very long.	— — — —	Stipitate plumose Calyx, unchanged.	233 Picris
	Inner, linear, converging outer, very short.		Stipitate, hairy Calyx converges roundish.	234 Crépis
Sect. IV. Neither imbricate calyculate, or Double.	Learlets equal. 8-leaved.	— — — —	Feathery, flat with about 32 rays.	235 Tragopógon
Sect. I. Flower capitate.	Learlets subequal, 10-leaved.	— — —	Hairy & calycled.	236 Hyoséris

Sect. II. All the Florets Tubular, (still the Polygamia æqualis of Linnæus.)

Imbricated globular.	Sect. I. armed with spines inflexed, hooked at the apex.	Chaffy, flat.	Sessile, very long.	237 Arctíum
ventricose.	Spines all straight & projecting sideways.	reticulated with scarred membranous cells like a honey-comb & somewhat chaffy.	capillary.	238 Onopórdum
— — — —	Spines imbricated only.	Hairy.	deciduous.	239 Cárduus
— — — —	Outer scales only armed, inner coloured, scariose, & radiant.	Chaffy.	plumose.	240 Carlína
nearly cylindrical.	Sect. II. unarmed, No Spines.	naked or chaffy.	sessile.	241 Serrátula
Sect. II. Flowers discoid Imbricated oblong.	linear-lanceolate unequal.	naked.	rough.	242 Eupatórium
— — — —	caniculate-concave often equal.	Chaffy, flat.	of 2 crowns.	243 Bídens
— — — —	ovate-oblong unequal.	___, flattish.	none.	244 Santolina

For Sect. III. Radiate flowers; i.e. Tubular florets in the Ray, or centre, & Ligulate in the Disk, or circumference, Vide Tab. 14. & 15.

London Published by Dr Thornton 1810

Clafs V. PENTANDRIA, continued.

DISCRIMINATING CHARACTERS.

Sect. III. Radiate Flowers. Tubular in the Ray & Ligulate Florets in the Difc.
(The Polygámia supérflua & frustránea of Linnæus.)

Forms of the Calyx	Flowers in the Circumference.	Scales of the Calyx.	Receptacle.	Pappus.	Genera.
Sect. I. Discoid. Hemispherical.	Few, 3-cleft, obscure, often none	acute, compact.	naked, convex.	somewhat marginate	245 Tanacétum.
roundifh.	———— ————	acute, th' outer ones spreading.	flat.	simple, rough.	246 Conýza.
————	No Corolla.	rounded, scariose, coloured.	naked.	simple.	247 Gnaphálium.
————	————	rounded converging	naked or villous.	rough or plumose.	248 Artemísia.

* Note. For Sect. II. Radiate. Corols of Ray Ligulate, Vide Tab. 15.

Davies fc.

London, Publifhed by Dr Thornton, 1812.

Clafs V. PENTANDRIA continued.

DISCRIMINATING CHARACTERS.

Sect. III. Radiate Flowers continued.

Form of Calyx.	Scales or Leaflets.	Florets of the Ray.	Receptacle.	Pappus.	Genera.
Sect. II. Radiate Hemispherical.	linear, nearly equal.	Females more than 5. in the ray, oblong.	Sect. I. Chaffy, conical.	marginate, or none.	249 Anthemis.
Imbricated.	ovate, acute, converging.	5 to 10 in the ray, roundish or abcordate.	elevated.	none.	250 Achillæa.
Hemispherical, erect.	10 to 20 placed in a double order, equal.	more numerous than the Calyx scales in the ray.	Sect. II. naked, conical.	------	251 Bellis.
Flat.	about 20 in a double order, equal, twice as long as the disk.	as many as the Calyx scales in the ray.	flat.	------	252 Doronicum.
Imbricated.	looser, patulous the outer ones larger equal.	numerous, crowded in the ray anthers with 2 bristles at the base in the bisexual flowers in the disk.	- - - -	simple, as long as the seed.	253 Innlá.
- - -	inner rather prominent at the apex, lower ones spreading.	------ more than 10 in the ray.	------ flattish.	hairy.	254 Aster.
Hemispherical.	linear, nearly equal, not scariose.	------ several.	------ convex.	none.	255 Matricária.
Hemispherical, imbricated.	closely incumbent, Inner gradually larger, scariose at the margin, mostly a scariose apex.	------ more than 12.	------ dotted.	marginate, or none.	256 Chrysánthemum.
Oblong, cylindrical, imbricated.	subular, erect, gradually longer, almost equal.	fewer than 10 generally 5.	flat.	long hairy.	257 Erigeron.
Oblong, imbricated.	oblong, narrow, acuminate, straight, converging.		flattish.	simple.	258 Solidágo.
simple many leaved.	Leaflets equal.	as many as the Calyx leaflets.		hairy, copious.	259 Cinerária.
Calycled, conical, truncated.	subulate, very numerous, parallel the tops, as if dead.	sometimes absent.	flat.	simple, long.	260 Senécio.
Cylindrical.	lanceolate, linear Berl equal, as long as the disk, somewhat membranous.	--	naked.	hairy, stipitate.	261 Tifsilágo.
Hemispherical, roundish.	sharpish, scariose at the base.	linear very numerous.		simple.	262 Pyréthrum.
Imbricated, roundish.	generally variously terminated.	Females fewer, large and loose in the dis. barren, being devoid of a Stigma.	bristly.	in most feathery, or hairy.	263 Centauréa.
simple, many leaved.	Leaves.	conspicuous.	naked, flat.	none.	264 Caléndula.

London. Published by Dr. Thornton, 1812.

Tab. 16.

Clafs V. PENTANDRIA, concluded.

DISCRIMINATING CHARACTERS.

Genera

		regular (*Stigma club-shaped*)	266. Jasione.
Set IV. Monogamia. *Flowers not compound but having the character of them as regards the Anthers.*	*Flowers 1-petalled*	irregular (*Stigma simple*)	266 Lobélia.
	5-petalled	Perianth 5-leaved	267 Violá.
		2-leaved	268 Impátiens.

London. Publifhed by D.r Thornton, June 4.1812.

Tab. 17.

Clafs VI. HEXANDRIA. Six Stamina.

DISCRIMINATING CHARACTERS.

Genera &
Exceptional
Species

			Corol. 5-petalled			269 Frankénia.
		Calyx, not a Spathe	Calyx 6-leaved			270 Bérberis.
	Sect. I. Flowers having a Corolla, and Calyx		6-petall'd	10-cleft		{ 1 Peplis Pórtul. Vide Gen. 286.
				12-cleft		{ 2 Lythrum Hyfsopifolium Vide Cl. II.
		a Spathe	A Nectary	of one leaf, petal-like, tubular		271 Narcifsus.
				3 leaves, emarginate		272 Galánthus.
			No Nectary	Petals thickened at the apex		273 Leucojum.
				No such Character		274 Allíum.
Order I. 1ogynia.		Corol. 1-petall'd	1 Stigma			275 Convallária.
	Sect. II. A Corolla, but No Calyx		3 Stigmata			276 Asparagús.
		6-petall'd	A Nectary	an hollow cup at the base of each petal		277 Fritillária.
				3 melliferous pores at the top of the germen		278 Hyacínthus.
			No Nectary	A Style	Stamens, filiform	Seeds round 279 Scílla.
						angular 280 Anthéricum.
					dilated at the base	281 Ornithógalum.
					hirsute	282 Narthécium.
				No Style	Flowers not inserted on a spadix 283 Tulipá.
					A Spadix	284 Acorús.
	Sect. III. No Corolla, but a Calyx	Calyx, 6-leaved.				285 Júncus.
		1-leaved, 12-cleft				286 Peplís.
Order II. Trigynia.	A Spathe					287 Colchicum.
	No Spathe	Corol. 3-petall'd	Seeds, capsuled			288 Triglochín
			naked. triquetrous			289 Rumere.
		6-petalled				290 Tofieldia.
Order III. Hygynia.						291 Alísma.

Order VIII. Tetradynamia, might come in here with propriety, but we have preferred
for the advantage of the tabular form to make it the concluding order —

Order IV. Adelphia	Calyx 2-leaved, Corolla ringent			292 Fumária.
Order V. Gynandria				293 Aristolóchia
Order VI. Monœcia	A Shrub			{ 3 Rumices Vide Gen. 289.
	A Tree			{ 4 Quercus Vide Cl. VIII.
Order VII. Diœcia	No Corolla			294 Tamus.
	A Corolla			{ 5 & 6 Rumex Acetosa & Acetosélla Vide Gen. 289.

London, Publifhed by Dr Thornton. 1812.

Class X. DECANDRIA, concluded.

DISCRIMINATING CHARACTERS.

Genera & Exceptional species

Plants remarkable for the following particulars.

1. Not formed of 2-petals — Banner reflexed; Legume long; filament adhering to the germen; stigma villous — 361 Spártium.
— erect; — short, scarcely longer than the calyx, inflated — 362 Uléx.

2. Stigma involute; the pistillum depressing the keel; banner reflexed, shorter than the keel; trifoliate — 363 Genísta.

3. Banner striated; legume rhomboid; banner cordate, longer than the wings; trifoliate — 364 Onónis.

4. Flowers capitate; erect at first, but depressed after impregnation; trifoliate — 365 Trifólium.

5. — umbelled — jointed — bowed only; round — 366 Ornithópus.
— incurved like an horse-shoe; one suture having many curved notches — 367 Hippocrépis.
not jointed; round, straight. Wings longer than the banner, converging upwards — 368 Lótus.

6. Legume taking a spiral form; trifoliate; keel gaping, released from the banner — 369 Medicágo.

7. Calyx inflated, including the legume; leaves pinnate, terminated by a larger leaflet; Flowers yellow or red in a double head — 370 Anthýllis.

8. Leaves pinnate, ending in an odd one — Legume bent into a curve, 2-celled — 371 Astragalús.
— straight — 372 Hedysárum.

9. Leaves pinnate, ending abruptly — Keel 2-cleft — Stigma linear, pubescent on the inner side from the middle to the top of the style — 373 Orobús.
— obtuse, transversely bearded under the summit — 374 Vícia.
— entire — Style keeled, stigma villous — 375 Písum.
flat; — — 376 Lathýrus.
simple; — beardless — 377 Érvum.

Order VII. Diœcia. — Calyx inflated, 3 Pistilla — 2 Cucubalus otítis. Vide Gen. 351.
— not inflated, 5 pistilla — 3 Lychnis. Vide Gen.

London, Published by Dr. Thornton, 1812.

Tab. 19.

Claſs VIII. OCTANDRIA, Eight Stamina.

DISCRIMINATING CHARACTERS.

Genera &
Exceptional Species.

Order I. Monogynia.	A Corolla	A Calyx	Calyx 4-toothed; Corolla 1-petalled	319 Vaccinium.
			— 4-cleft; ——— 4-petalled	320 Epilóbium.
			— 8-parted	321 Clóra.
			— 4-leaved	322 Erica.
		No Calyx		{1 Monótropa hypopithis Vide Cl. X.
	No Corolla			323 Daphne.
Order II. Digynia.	Calyx superior, lateral flowers having 8 Stamina			{2 Chrysosplénium oppositifolium, Vide G. 346.
	——— inferior			{3 Scleranthus Vide Cl. X
Order III. Trigynia.				324 Polygonum.
Order IV. Tetragynia.	1-petalled			325 Adóxa.
	4-petalled	A Berry		326 Páris.
		A Capsule		327 Elatina.
Order V. adelphia.	Calyx 5-leaved			328 Polygala.
Order VI. Monœcia.	An herb			329 Myriophyllum.
	Tree or Shrub	Calyx 4 or 5-cleft, (Male) ——— entire (Female flower)		330 Quércus.
		——— 3-cleft (Male) ——— 2-cleft (Female ———)		331 Corylus.
		——— ciliate		332 Carpinus.
Order VII. Diœcia.	An herb			333 Rhodíola.
	A Tree	A Corolla		334 Populus.
		No Corolla		{4 Salix pentandra Vide Cl. II.
Order VIII. Polygamia.	Flowers bisexual, with some Male flowers on the same plant			335 Acer.

Claſs IX. ENNEANDRIA. Nine Stamina.

Order I. Monogynia.	No Calyx (6 petals)		336 Butomus.
Order II. Diœcia.	A Corolla (an aquatic)		337 Hydrocháris.
	No Corolla		338 Mercuriális.

Tab 20.

Class X. DECANDRIA, Ten Stamina.

DISCRIMINATING CHARACTERS.

Genera &
Exceptional Species

Order I.

Monogynia

- Flowers 1-petalled
  - A Capsule .... 339 Andromeda.
  - A Berry
    - 5-celled .... 340 Arbutus.
    - 4 .... { Vaccinium Myrtillus et uliginosum. Vide a.VII.
- Several petals
  - Petals 5 .... 341 Monotropa.
  - 10 .... 342 Pyrola.

Order II.

Digynia

- A Corolla
  - Scales at the base of the Calyx .... 343 Dianthus.
  - No such character
    - Petals upright .... 344 Saponaria.
    - spreading .... 345 Saxifraga.
- No Corolla
  - Calyx spreading, coloured .... 346 Chrysoplenium.
  - tubular .... 347 Scleranthus.

Order III.

Trigynia

- A Corolla
  - entire .... 348 Arenaria.
  - 2-cleft or 2-parted
    - spreading .... 349 Stellaria.
    - upright
      - Berry 1-celled .... 350 Cucubalus.
      - Capsule 3-celled .... 351 Silene.
- No Corolla .... 352 Cherleria.

Order IV.

Pentagynia

- Calyx 1-leaved
  - 1-petalled .... 353 Cotyledon.
  - 5-petalled
    - Calyx spreading .... 354 Sedum.
    - tubular
      - membranous .... 355 Lychnis.
      - coriaceous .... 356 Agrostemma.
- 5-leaved
  - Petals connected at the base .... 357 Oxalis.
  - No such character
    - bifid .... 358 Cerastium.
    - entire .... 359 Spergula
    - .... 360 Geranium.

For the other Orders Monodelphia, Diadelphia, & Dioecia, Vide Tab. 2?

London. Published by Dr. Thornton. Jan. 1812.

Clafs X. DECANDRIA, concluded.

DISCRIMINATING CHARACTERS.

Genera &
Exceptional Species

Plants remarkable for the following particulars.

Tetr. elphia and &phia. wers iaceous]

1. Keel formed of 2-petals
- {Banner reflexed; Legume long; filament adhering to the germen; stigma villous.} — 361 Spártium.
- {—— erect; —— short, scarcely longer than the Calyx, inflated.} — 362 Uléx.

2. Stigma involute; the pistillum deprefsing the keel; banner reflexed, shorter than the keel; trifoliate — 363 Genísta.

3. Banner striated; legume rhomboid; banner cordate, longer than the wings; trifoliate — 364 Onónis.

4. Flowers capitate; erect at first, but deprefsed after impregnation; trifoliate — 365 Trifólium.

5. —— umbelled
- jointed
  - {bowed only; round — 366 Ornithópus.
  - {incurved like an horse-shoe; one suture having many curved notches.} — 367 Hippocrépis.
- {not jointed; round, straight. Wings longer than the banner, converging upwards.} — 368 Lótus.

6. Legume taking a spiral form; trifoliate; keel gaping, reflexed from the banner — 369 Medicágo.

7. Calyx inflated, including the legume; leaves pinnate, terminated by a larger leaflet; Flowers yellow or red in a double head.} — 370 Anthýllis.

8. Leaves pinnate, ending in an odd one
- {Legume bent into a curve, 2-celled — 371 Astragalús.
- —— straight — 372 Hedysárum.

9. Leaves pinnate, ending abruptly
- Keel 2-cleft
  - {Stigma linear, pubescent on the inner side from the middle to the top of the style.} — 373 Orobús.
  - {—— obtuse, transversely bearded under the summit} — 374 Vícia.
- entire
  - {Style keeled, stigma villous — 375 Písum.
  - —— flat; — —— — 376 Lathýrus.
  - —— simple; —— beardlefs — 377 Ervum.

Order VII. Diœcia.
- {Calyx inflated, 3 Pistilla — {2 Cucubalus otites. Vide Gen 351.
- —— not inflated, 5 pistilla — {3 Lychnis ?... Vide Gen ...

London, Published by Dr. Thornton, 1812.

Tab. 22.

Clafs XI. DODECANDRIA, 12 to 20 Stamina.

DISCRIMINATING CHARACTERS.

		Genera & *Exceptional Species*
Order I. monogynia.	{ A Corolla, 6-petalled, Calyx 3-cleft, superior.	578 Asarum.
	{ No Corolla. ————— 1² cleft, inferior.	379 Lythrum.
Order II. digynia.	} Petals 5, inserted in the Calyx.	580 Agrimonia.
Order III. trigynia.	{ Germen simple, filaments 11 or 15, Petals several of them half 3 cleft.	581 Reseda
	{ ———— pedicelled. ———— 12 or more, ———— 4 or 5, truncated.	382 Euphorbia.
Order IV. tetragynia.	} Calyx 12-parted; Corol. 12-petalled; Stamina 12; Pistilla 12; Capsules 12.	583 Sempervivum.
Order V. monœcia.	} Calyx many-parted; an aquatic.	584 Ceratophyllum.
Order VI. diœcia.	} Calyx 3-parted; Corolla none; Stamina 9 or 12.	{ Mercurialis perennis *Vide tab 558.*

r.

London, Publifhed by Dr Thornton, 1812

Tab. 23.

Claſs XII. POLYANDRIA, 20 or more Stamina.

DISCRIMINATING CHARACTERS.

Genera &
Exceptional Species.

Sat. I.
a inserted
Receptacle.
Monandria
innixus.;

Corol. 4-petalled —
2-leaved —
A Capsule covered with a radiated stigma, rising so as to form many holes .... 385 Papáver.
A Silique —
1-celled .... 386 Chelidónium.
2 ___ ____ .... 387 Gláucium.

4 _____ .... 388 Actǽa.

Order I.
Trigynia.

5-petalled —
1-leaved; 5-parted, deciduous; capsule 5-valved, opening at the base .... 389 Tiliá.
5 ___ 2 leaves, less than the others; capsule 5-valved, opening at top .... 390 Ciſtus.

many-petalled; Calyx larger than the petals; berry many-celled .... 391 Nymphǽa.

Order III.
Trigynia.

A Calyx .... { 1 Reseda luteola. Vide Gen. 381.

No Calyx —
Nectary sessile .... { 2 Helleborus. Vide Gen. 399.
___ pedicelled, resembling 2 elevated Dolphins .... 392 Delphínium.

Order IV.
Trigynia.

Nectaries 5, horned, so as to resemble a nest of Doves .... 393 Aquilégia.

Order V.
Trigynia.

Spathe 2-leaved; Perianth trifid; Petals 3, (an aquatic) .... 394 Stratiótes.

Order VI.
Polygynia.

A Calyx —
No Nectary; petals 5 to 10 —
An Involucre .... 395 Anémone.
No Involucre .... 396 Adónis.
A Nectary at the unguis of the 5 petals .... 397 Ranúnculus.

No Calyx —
Petals 5, largest, stem 2 or 3 feet high —
No Nectary; leaves heart-shaped .... 398 Cáltha.
Nectary tubular, sessile; leaves lobed .... 399 Helléborus.

4 to 6 —
Seed, without a tail (Petals 4, rarely 5 or 6) .... 400 Thalíctrum.
___ caudate; stem climbing (Petals usually 4) .... 401 Clématis.
14. Nectary linear, petal-like .... 402 Tróllius.

Order VII.
Polyadelphia.

A double Calyx, outer 1-leaved —
3-cleft .... 403 Lavatéra.
9-cleft .... 404 Málva.
___ ___ 3-leaved .... 405 Althǽa.

Order VIII.
Polyadelphia.

Calyx 5-parted; petals 5; filaments coalesced in 3 or 5 parcels .... 406 Hypéricum.

Order IX.
Monœcia.

Calyx of the male flower, 3-leaved; stamens about 24 .... 407 Sagittária.
___ ___ 4-leaved; ___ 30 to 40 .... 408 Potérium.
___ ___ scales, resembling a bud .... 409 Pínus.

Order X.
Diœcia.

An aquatic, a plant; Corolla 3-petalled .... { 3 Stratiótes Aloides. Vide Gen. 394.
A Tree —
A Corolla .... { 4 Populus nigra. Vide Gen. 334.
No Corolla .... 410 Taxus.

London. Published by Dr Thornton, 1812.

DISCRIMINATING CHARACTERS.

Genera &
Exceptional Species.

Sect. II.
are inserted
in the Calyx.
(Icosandria
of Linnæus.)

Order I.
Monogynia.

Calyx 5-cleft, beneath .... 411 Prúnus.

‒ ‒ ‒ ‒ , above .... { 5 Méspilus oxycántha. *Vide Gen.* 412

Order II.
Digynia.

A Drupe .... 6 Méspilus oxycántha.

A Pome .... { 7 Pyrus torminális hybrica & aria. *Vide Gen.* 413.

Order III.
Trigynia.

A Drupe .... 8 Méspilus oxycántha.

A Pome .... { 9 Pyrus torminális aucuparia hybrida & aria.

Order IV.
Tetragynia.

A Pome .... { 10 Pyrus torminális aucuparia & aria.

Order V.
Pentagynia.

Calyx above ‒

A Drupe .... 412 Méspilus.

A Pome .... 413 Pýrus.

‒‒‒‒ beneath, a Capsule .... 414 Spiróea.

Order VI.
Polygynia.

Calyx 5-cleft ‒

urn-shaped at bottom, with 5 segments above, 3 of them fringed, turning to a fruit .... 415 Rósa.

No such base, but 5 spreading leaflets, fruit an acinus, or compound berry ‒ ..... 416 Rúbus.

A Capsule .... { 11 Spiróea filipéndula et ulmaria. *Vide Gen.* 414.

‒‒‒‒ 8-cleft, Corolla 4-petalled .... 417 Tormentílla.

‒‒‒‒ 8 or 10-cleft, ‒‒‒‒ 5 or 8 petalled .... 418 Drýas.

10-cleft ‒

Seed naked affixed to a berried receptacle .... 419 Fragária

‒‒‒‒‒, armed with a long crown, which is geniculate or kneed ..... 420 Géum.

‒‒‒‒‒, crownlefs, rugose .... 421 Potentílla.

‒‒‒‒‒ ‒‒‒‒‒, smooth .... 422 Comárum.

London, Publifhed by Dr Thornton, 1812.

SPECIES of BRITISH PLANTS.

CLASS I. MONANDRIA.

DISCRIMINATING CHARACTERS.

Order I. Monogynia.

	Species
1. Salicornia. *(Salt-wort.)*	**Salicórnia.**
compressed, emarginate; stem soft; spikes peduncled	**1. Herbácea.** *(Herbaceous)*
cylindrical, entire; stem ligneous; spiked almost sessile	**2. Fruticósa.** *(Shrubby)*
1. Hippúris. *(Mares-tail.)*	**Hippúris.**
Leaves verticillate, linear	**3. Vulgáris.** *(Common)*

Order II. Digynia.

1. Callitriche. *(Star-wort.)*	**Callítriche.**
Leaves, upper, in form of a Star	**4. Aquática.** *(Aquatic.)*

Order III. Gynandria.

1. Arum. *(Cuckow-pint.)*	**Árum.**
Leaves, arrow-shaped	**5. Maculátum.** *(Spotted.)*
5. Zostéra. *(Grafs-wrack.)*	**Zostéra.**
Leaves growing under water, & floating with the tide	**6. Marina.** *(Marine.)*

Order IV. Monœcia.

6. Zannichéllia. *(Pond-weed.)*	**Zannichéllia.**
Leaves linear, grafsy, subverticillate	**7. Palústris.** *(Marsh.)*
7. Chára. *(Chara.)*	**Chára.**
armed; prickles setaceous, deflexed	**8. Híspida.** *(Hispid.)*
unarmed { smooth, transparent	**9. Fléxilis.** *(Flexile.)*
striated, opake	**10. Vulgáris.** *(Common.)*

London. Publifhed by D. Thornton, 1812.

CLASS II. DIANDRIA.

DISCRIMINATING CHARACTERS.

					Species
Order I. Monogynia.					
6.t. Ligústrum. *(Privet.)*					**Ligústrum.**
Leaves. elliptic-lanceolate. dagger-pointed					11. Vulgáre. *(Common.)*
6.9. Verónica. *(Veronica.)* Sect. I. Flowers solitary					**Verónica.**

Leaves
- ovate
  - Stems procumbent .... 12 Agréstis. *(Meadow.)*
  - ___ erect .... 13 Arvénfis. *(Field.)*
- cordate, 5-lobed .... 14 Hederifólia. *(Ivy-leaved.)*
- digitate-parted
  - Peduncles longer than the Calyx .... 15 Triphyllos. *(Three-leaved.)*
  - _____ shorter ___ ___ ___ .... 16 Verna. *(Spring.)*

Sect. II. Spiked.

Spikes
- terminal
  - Stem, ascending .... 17 Spicáta. *(Spiked.)*
  - ___ nearly erect .... 18 Hýbrida. *(Hybrid.)*
- lateral, ___ procumbent .... 19 Officinális. *(Officinal.)*

Sect. III. Corymbosed.

corymbus
- terminal, few-flowered: stem diffuse .... 20 Saxátilis. *(Rock.)*
- _____ many-flowered; ___ erect .... 21 Fruticulósa. *(Shrubby.)*
- _____ somewhat spiked; ___ ascending .... 22 Alpína. *(Alpine.)*

Sect. IV. Racemed.

Racemes
- terminal .... 23 Serpyllifólia. *(Thyme-leaved.)*
- lateral
  - Leaves, elliptical, stem creeping .... 24 Beccabúnga. *(Water.)*
  - ___ lanceolate; ___ erect .... 25 Anagállis. *(Pimpernel-like.)*
  - ___ linear .... 26 Scutelláta. *(Shielded.)*
  - ___ ovate
    - petioled: stem all hairy .... 27 Montána. *(Mountain.)*
    - sefsile. ___ hairy bifariously .... 28 Chamædris. *(Germander-like.)*

m. 10. Pinguícula. *(Butterwort.)* .... **Pinguícula.**

Nectary
- obtuse, shorter than the petal .... 29 Lusitánica. *(Portuguese.)*
- acute, length of the petal .... 30 Vulgáris. *(Common.)*

m. 11. Utriculária. *(Milfoil.)* .... **Utriculária.**

Nectary
- conical .... 31 Vulgáris. *(Common.)*
- keeled .... 32 Minor. *(Lefs.)*

London. Published by D.r Thornton, 1812.

Clafs II. DIANDRIA, Continued.

DISCRIMINATING CHARACTERS.

Species.

No. 12. Sálvia. (Sage.) .... Sálvia.

leaves { crenate: Corolla twice as big as the Calyx, ... 33. Praténsis.
(Meadow.)

serrate; _____ only once as big: .... 34. Verbenáca.
(Vervain-leaved.)

No. 13. Verbéna. (Vervain.) .... Verbéna.
Leaves multifid-laciniated .... 35. Officinalis.
(Officinal.)

No. 14. Lycopus. (Gypsy-wort.) .... Lycopus.
Leaves sinuate-serrated .... 36. Europǽus.
(European.)

No. 15 Circǽa. (Enchanters-Night-shade.) .... Circǽa.

leaves { ovate; Stem erect .... 37. Lutetiána.
(Common.)

cordate; _____ ascending .... 38. Alpína.
(Alpine.)

Order II. Digynia.

No. 16. Anthoxánthum. (Vernal grafs.) .... Anthoxánthum
Spike ovate-oblong .... 39. Odorátum.
(Sweet.)

Order III Gynandria.

No. 17. Orchis. (Orchis.) .... Orchis.

Sect. I. Bulbs undivided.

very entire .... 40. Bifólia.
(Two-leaved.)

3-cleft .... 41. Pyramidális.
(Pyramidal.)

of the nectary { 4-cleft { Spur, half the length of the Germen, or nearly so .... 42. Ustuláta.
(Dwarf.)

_____ as long as the Germen, or nearly so { Outer Petals converging .... 43. Mório.
(Buffoon.)

_____ _____ open, reflexed .... 44. Máscula.
(Male.)

5-cleft .... 45. Militáris.
(Military.)

Sect. II. Bulbs palmated.

of the nectary { twice as long as the Germen .... 46. Conópsea.
(Fly.)

shorter than the Germen { Stem solid, leaves spotted .... 47. Maculáta.
(Spotted.)

_____ fistulous, leaves green, broad .... 48. Latifólia.
(Broad-leaved.)

No. 18. Satýrium. (Satyrion.) .... Satýrium.

Root { fibrous, creeping .... 49. Repéns.
(Creeping.)

bulbous { Nectary 3 cleft, middle Segment very short .... 50. Víride.
(Green.)

_____ _____ very long { linear, twisted .... 51. Hircínum.
(Goat.)

ending acute, straight ...... 52. Albídum.
(White.)

London, Published by Dr Thornton, 1812.

Davis fc.

Clafs II. DIANDRIA, continued.

DISCRIMINATING CHARACTERS.

Species.

 19. Ophrys. (Ophrys.)..**Ophrys.**

Sect. I. Bulbs branched.

Leaves — two — ovate Lip of the Nectary 2-cleft......................53. Ovàta.
(Ovate)

cordate; — — 4-lobed......................54. Cordàta.
(Cordate)

none — lip of the Nectary 2-cleft; root fascicled......................55. Nìdus Àvis.
(Birds-nest)

— — — entire; — branched, twisted......................56. Corállorhìza.
(Coral-rooted)

Sect. II. Bulbs oblong.

Spike curiously twisted......................57. Spirális.
(Spiral)

Sect. III. Bulbs round.

Bulb — single, Nectary 3-cleft......................58. Monórchis.
(Single-bulbed)

two — — 4-cleft; petals converging......................59. Anthropóphora.
(Man)

— 5-cleft; — erect coloured......................60. Apífera.
(Bee)

— 6-cleft; — — —......................61. Muscífera.
(Fly)

— obscurely cleft, & rounded like the bee; Petals erect, green......................62. Aranífera.
(Spider)

20. Serápias. (Serapias.)......................**Serápias.**

Flowers — drooping — Lip of the Nectary entire, shorter than the petals......................63. Latifòlia.
(Broad-leaved)

— — — crenate, equal to the petals......................64. Palústris.
(Marsh)

erect — Petals bent back, purple......................65. Rùbra.
(Red)

unflexed, white — lip as short again as the petals......................66. Ensifòlia.
(Sword-leaved)

— nearly the length of the — —......................67. Grandiflòra.
(Large-flowering)

21. Cypripèdium. (Ladies-slipper.)......................**Cypripèdium.**

Root fibrous; Stem leafy......................68. Calcéolus.
(Ladies-slipper)

22. Maláxis. (Tway-blade.)......................**Maláxis.**

Leaves spatulate rough at the apex; Stem 5-sided......................69. Paludòsa.
(Marshy)

Order IV. Monœcia.

23. Lémna. (Duck's-meat.)......................**Lémna.**

Leaves — petioled......................70. Trisúlca.
(Three-furrowed)

sessile — Root single — Leaf flattish on both sides......................71. Mìnor.
(Left)

— rather convex......................72. Gibba.
(Gibbous)

— crowded......................73. Polyrrhìza.
(Much-rooted)

London. Publifhed by D.Thornton, 1812.

Clafs II. DIANDRIA, continued.

DISCRIMINATING CHARACTERS.

Order V. Diœcia.	Species
24. Sálix (Willow)	Sálix.

Sect. I. Leaves smoothish, margins entire.

Leaves reticulated with veins .... 74 Reticuláta. *(Knetted)*

Sect. II. Leaves smoothish, margins cut.

Sect. I. Flowers androus.

Stem decumbent, twigs red .... 75 Púrpurea. *(Purple)*

erect — Leaves obovate-lanceolate; stigma emarginate .... 76 Lambertiána. *(Lambert's)*

lanceolate — bluish beneath .... 77 Monándra. *(One-Stamen'd)*

glaucous beneath .... 78 Forbyána. *(Forbs)*

Sect. II. androus.

Leaves orbicular, veins yellow, a diminutive tree .... 79 Herbácea. *(Herbaceous)*

ovate — denticulated, compressed, finely veined, forming a keel .... 80 Carináta. *(Keeled)*

serrated — reticulated with veins above .... 81 Venulósa. *(Veiny)*

even above .... 82 Prunifólia. *(Plum-leaved)*

elliptical — Shining on both sides, serrated, veiny .... 83 Myrsinites. *(Whortle-leaved)*

obscurely denticulated .... 84 Dicksoniána. *(Dicksons)*

glaucous beneath — denticulate-serrated .... 85 Bicólor. *(Two-coloured)*

serrated .... 86 Tenuifólia. *(Slender-leaved)*

elliptic-lanceolate — crenate .... 87 Nígricans. *(Black)*

unequally crenate; branches decumbent, rooting .... 88 Rádicans. *(Rooting)*

elliptic-oblong, toothed, repand, scariose .... 89 Malifólia. *(Apple-leaved)*

lanceolate — undulated; stipules sublunate .... 90 Phylicifólia. *(Tea-leaved)*

obscurely lenticulate; no stipule .... 91 Arbúscula. *(Shrub-like)*

serrated — Serratures cartilagenous .... 92 Lútea. *(Yellow)*

Petioles covered with glands .... 93 Frágilis. *(Fragile)*

Stigma sessile, 2 lobed .... 94 Petioláris. *(Petiolate)*

Sect. III. Triandrous.

Leaves linear-oblong .... 95 Triándria. *(Three-Stamen'd)*

ovate; Stipules very large .... 96 Amygdalina. *(Almond-leaved)*

lanceolate — Petioles decurrent .... 97 Lanceoláta. *(Lanceolate)*

No such character .... 98 Rufselliána. *(Bufsel)*

Sect. IV. ntandrous.

Leaves elliptic-lanceolate .... 99 Pentándra. *(Five-Stamen'd)*

Sect. V. nadelphous.

Leaves linear-lanceolate, denticulate, green on both sides .... 100 Rúbra. *(Red)*

elliptical, slightly serrated, glaucous beneath .... 101 Croweána. *(Crows)*

London, Published by Dr. Thornton, 1812.

DISCRIMINATING CHARACTERS.

Species.

Sect. III. Leaves, villous, margins entire. **Sálix**

de-acute, somewhat villous above, clothed with very dense wool beneath...............102. **Arenária.**
(Mountain.)

nate-lanceolate, glaucous, & somewhat villous, with reticulated veins beneath, stipulæ semi-cordate, serrated.103. **Cinerea.**
(Grey.)

volate-linear, very long, acuminate, very entire, silky beneath: branches rod-like; style elongated..............104. **Viminális.**
(Common Osier.)

Elliptical { ending acute; stem prostrate; leaves slightly toothed, glaucous & silky beneath..........105. **Prostráta.**
(Prostrate.)

{ —— with a small hooked point; rather villous above, silky & shining beneath; } 106. **Argéntea.**
as well as the twigs. } *(Silvery.)*

{ —— as if dead at the apex; leaves flat...............107. **Spacelata.**
(Withered.)

nte-lanceolate; somewhat dagger-pointed; rather naked above, glaucous or silky beneath; stem depreffed 108. **Repens.**
(Creeping.)

ar-lanceolate, straight, silky beneath; stem erect; stipulæ erect, flat ....109. **Rosmarinifólia.**
(Rosemary-leaved.)

Sect. IV. Leaves villous, margins cut.

te, acuminate, serrated, undulated; tomentous beneath; stipulæ sub-lunate.................110. **Cáprea.**
(Goat's.)

te, somewhat serrated, obtuse, with a small hooked point, villous & reticulated } ....111. **Aurita.**
with veins on both sides; stipulæ various. } *(Round-eared.)*

—elliptical, somewhat serrated, pubescent, flat; somewhat glaucous beneath; stipulæ rounded, toothed......112. **Aquatica.**
(Common Aquatic.)

—lanceolate, flat, denticulated, acute, glaucous & hairy beneath; stipulæ small ....113. **Oleifólia.**
(Olive-leaved.)

t orbicular, obscurely toothed; villous, marked with rectangular veins beneath...............114. **Cotinifólia.**
(Quince-leaved.)

ic-cordate, acuminate, finely notched, pubescent on both sides; stipulæ semi-cordate, flat, } 115. **Hirta.**
toothed, nearly smooth; branches hairy. } *(Hairy.)*

olate { stipules semi-cordate, very large; leaves acuminate, obscurely crenate; } ....116. **Stipuláris.**
tomentous beneath, nectary cylindrical. } *(Stipuled.)*

{ —— lunate, very small; leaves acuminate, subcrenate, whitish & silky beneath..........117. **Mollíssima.**
(Silky.)

{ —— none; leaves acuminate, serrated, silky on both sides; the lowest } 118. **Alba.**
serratures glandular, stigma. 2-parted. } *(Common White.)*

t-oblong { kidney-shaped; leaves somewhat denticulated, acute; smooth above, } ....119. **Fúsca.**
glaucous & silky beneath; petioles attenuated. } *(Brown.)*

{ —— hardly perceptible; leaves acuminate, undulated, toothed, downy beneath..........120. **Acumináta.**
(Pointed.)

ts. **Fráxinus.** *(Ash.)* ....**Fráxinus.**

es pinnated, pinnæ serrated ....121. **Excélsior.**
(Lofty.)

. Where the discriminations were thought difficult, we have joined with them several other characters.

London, Publifhed by Dr. Thornton, 1811.

Tab. 7. *

Claſs III. TRIANDRIA.

DISCRIMINATING CHARACTERS.

Order I. Monogynia.   Species

n. 26. Valeriána. (*Valerian.*) .... Valeriána.

l: ers { monandrous .... 122 Rubra.
                                                                              (*Red.*)
        { triandrous { Flowers dioicous .... 123 Dióica.
                                                                              (*Diœcious.*)
                     { not dioicous { Leaves pinnatifid .... 124 Officinális.
                                                                              (*Officinal.*)
                                    { ____ not pinnatifid .... 125 Locúſta.
                                                                              (*Sallad.*)

n 27 Crócus (*Crocus.*) .... Crócus.

igmata { projecting, 3-parted .... 126 Sativus.
                                                                              (*Saffron.*)
       { enclosed, trifid { divisions incised .... 127 Vérnus.
                                                                              (*Vernal.*)
                          { ____ pencilled .... 128 Núdi-florus.
                                                                              (*Naked-flowered.*)

n 28 Iris (*Flag.*) .... Iris.

ner Petals { leſs than the Stigmata, erect .... 129 Pseúdacórus.
                                                                              (*Acorus-like.*)
           { larger ___ ___ _____, spreading .... 130 Fœtidíſsima.
                                                                              (*Most Fœtid.*)

l 29 Nárdus (*Mat-graſs*) .... Nárdus

Spike 1-rowed .... 131 Stricta.
                                                                              (*Upright.*)

l 30 Erióphorum (*Cotton Graſs*) .... Erióphorum

Culm { angular. naked .... 132 Alpínum.
                                                                              (*Alpine.*)
     { round. sheathed { Spike with a solitary flower ... 133 Vaginátum.
                                                                              (*Sheathed.*)
                        { ____ several { Leaves flat ...... 134 Polystáchion.
                                       { ____ channelled ... 135 Angustifólium
                                                                              (*Narrow-leaved.*)

31 Schœnus (*Bog-rush*) .... Schœnus

leafy { Leaves setaceous .... 136 Albus.
                                                                              (*White.*)
      { ____ prickly on the back & margin .... 137 Mariscus.

naked { head ovate. involucre 2-leaved .... 138 Nigricans.
                                                                              (*Black.*)
      { ____ spike 2-rowed { shorter than the 1-leaved involucre ... 139 Compréſsus.
                                                                              (*Compreſsed.*)
                            { longer ___ ___ ___ ___ ... 140 Rufus.
                                                                              (*Brown.*)

l. 32 Cypérus (*Cyperus.*) .... Cypérus

Culm. 3-sided, leafy .... 141 Lóngus.
                                                                              (*Long.*)

London. Publiſhed by Dr. Thornton. 1812.

DISCRIMINATING CHARACTERS.

(Club-rush) .... **Scírpus**

Sect. I Spikes, single & terminal.

the water, leafy, & branched .... 142 Fluitans.
(Floating.)

{quadrangular .... 143 Aciculáris.
(Needle-like.)

ter { round { few-flowered (under 5) .... 144 Pauciflórus.
(Few-flowered.)

{ many { Glumes acute .... 145 Palústris.
(Marsh.)

{ obtuse { both equal .... 146 Multicáulis.
(Many-culmed.)

{ the exterior, largest .... 147 Cœspitósus.
(Turfy.)

Sect. II Spikes, several.

several feet high { Spike oval .... 148 Lacústris.
(Larger Bull-rush.)

{ round .... 149 Holoschœnus.
(Round-headed Bull-rush.)

only a few inches .... 150 Setáceus.
(Setaceous.)

panicle naked .... 151 Triquéter.
(Triangular.)

{ Glumes mucronated .... 152 Marítimus.
(Salt marsh.)

leafy { ending obtuse .... 153 Sylváticus.
(Wood.)

Order II Digynia.

(Panick-Grafs) .... **Pánicum**

spikelets in fours, involucre 1flowered, 2-bristled .... 154 Verticillátum.
(Verticillate.)

crowded, 2flowered, many-bristled .... 155 Viridé.
(Green.)

alternate, or in pairs .... 156 Crus gálli.
(Cock's-foot.)

flowers in pairs .... 157 Sanguinále.
(Sanguineous.)

single, runners creeping .... 158 Dactylon.
(Digitate.)

(Fox-tail grafs) .... **Alopecúrus**

paniculate, spike somewhat lobed .... 159 Geniculátus.
(Kneed.)

es, nakedish, spike very simple, root fibrous .... 160 Agréstis.
(Field.)

{ Spike somewhat lobed .... 161 Praténsis.
(Meadow.)

villous { very simple, pointed, root bulbous .... 162 Bulbósus.
(Bulbous.)

{ ovate .... 163 Alpínus.
(Alpine.)

London. Publifhed by Dr Thornton, 1812.

Clafs III. TRIANDRIA, continued.

DISCRIMINATING CHARACTERS.

1.33 Scirpus *(Club-rush)* .... **Scirpus**

Sect. I Spikes, single & terminal.

floating on the water, leafy, & branched .... 142 **Fluitans.** *(Floating.)*

tem { no such character {

quadrangular .... 143 **Acicularis.** *(Needle-like.)*

round { few-flowered (under 5) .... 144 **Pauciflorus.** *(Few-flowered.)*

many { Glumes acute .... 145 **Palustris.** *(Marsh.)*

obtuse { both equal .... 146 **Multicaulis.** *(Many-culmed.)*

the exterior, largest .... 147 **Cœspitosus.** *(Turfy.)*

Sect. II Spikes, several.

cylindrical { several feet high { Spike oval .... 148 **Lacustris.** *(Larger Bull-rush.)*

round .... 149 **Holoschœnus.** *(Round-headed Bull-rush.)*

only a few inches .... 150 **Setaceus.** *(Setaceous.)*

3-sided { panicle naked .... 151 **Triquéter.** *(Triangular.)*

leafy { Glumes mucronated .... 152 **Maritimus.** *(Salt marsh.)*

ending obtuse .... 153 **Sylváticus.** *(Wood.)*

Order II Digynia.

34 Pánicum *(Panick-Grafs)* .... **Pánicum**

verticillate, spikelets in fours, involucre 1-flowered, 2-bristled .... 154 **Verticillátum.** *(Verticillate.)*

cylindrical, — crowded, — 2-flowered, many-bristled .... 155 **Viridé.** *(Green.)*

decomposed, — alternate, or in pairs .... 156 **Crus gálli.** *(Cock's-foot.)*

digitate { flowers in pairs .... 157 **Sanguinále.** *(Sanguineous.)*

single, runners creeping .... 158 **Dactylon.** *(Digitate.)*

35 Alopecúrus *(Fox-tail grafs)* .... **Alopecúrus**

ascending, geniculate, spike somewhat lobed .... 159 **Geniculátus.** *(Kneed.)*

erect { Glumes, nakedifh, spike very simple, root fibrous .... 160 **Agréftis.** *(Field.)*

villous { Spike somewhat lobed .... 161 **Praténsis.** *(Meadow.)*

very simple, pointed, root bulbous .... 162 **Bulbósus.** *(Bulbous.)*

ovate .... 163 **Alpínus.** *(Alpine.)*

London, Publifhed by Dr Thornton, 1812.

Tab. 9 *

Clafs III. TRIANDRIA, continued.

DISCRIMINATING CHARACTERS.

Species

n. 36. Phléum *(Cat's-tail grafs)* .... **Phléum**

nite { *very long (1 or more inches) Glumes longer than the Crowns* .... 164 **Pratense.**
(Field)

{ *not so long (lefs than an inch)* .... *shorter* .... 165 **Alpinum.**
(Alpine)

nide { *Spiked ; glumes naked ; no Crowns* .... 166 **Paniculatum.**
(Panicled)

{ *Spike like ;* .... *bispid ;Crowns very long* .... 167 **Crinitum.**
(Bearded)

n. 37. Phaláris *(Canary Grafs.)* .... **Phaláris**

Spike ovate-lanceolate, obtuse culm branched from the base, in the others simple .... 168 **Arenaria.**
(Sandy.)

nide { *ovate; Calyx-glumes, white, boat-shaped keel smooth ; Corolla 4-valved* .... 169 **Canariensis.**
(Canary,)

{ *nearly round ; Calyx-glumes, ovate-linear ;* ____ *pubefcent,* ____ *2-valved* .... 170 **Phleoides.**
(Cats-tail)

n. 38. Milium *(Millet)* .... **Milium**

nide { *somewhat spiked ; Flowers crowned* .... 171 **Lendigerum.**
(Amber seeded.)

{ *diffuse ;* _____ *crownlefs* .... 172 **Effusum.**
(Diffuse.)

en. 39. Dactýlis *(Cock's-foot grafs.)* .... **Dactýlis**

ters { *spiked ; in pairs, erect, smooth ; 1 rowed ; Stem smooth* .... 173 **Stricta.**
(Erect.)

{ *panicled ; branched alternately ; conglomerate ;* ____ *rough* .... 174 **Glomerata.**
(Glomerate.)

en. 40. Stipa *(Feather Grafs)* .... **Stipa**

Crown feathered, near a foot in length .... 175 **Pennáta.**
(Downy.)

en. 41. Lagúrus *(Hairs-tail grafs)* .... **Lagúrus**

Spike ovate .... 176 **Ovatus.**
(Ovate.)

en. 42. Aira *(Hair Grafs)* .... **Aira**

Sect. 1. Crowned.

{ *3 or 4 feet high: Leaves smooth flat ; Glumes villous at the base ; Crowns short, straight* .... 177 **Cæfpitosa.**
(Turfy.)

ten { Panicle compact { *Floscules hairy at the base, some of these pedicelled ; Crown clavate at the apex, shorter than the Calyx of a grey colour)* .... 178 **Canescens.**
(Grey.)

from 3 inches to a foot high. Leaves setaceous { .... *naked at the base, sessile ; Crown geniculate, twice as long as the Calyx.* } .... 179 **Præcox.**
(Early,)

{ spreading { ____ *pedunculed, peduncules twisted ; Stem almost naked ; Panicle whitish-purple.* } .... 180 **Flexuosa**
(Twisted.)

{ ____ *sessile ; Stem leafy ; Panicle a silvery-purple* .... 181 **Argentéa.**
(Silver.)

Sect. II. Crownlefs.

nide { *compact ; Leaves linear, rough* .... 182 **Cristáta.**
(Crefted.)

{ *spreading ;* ____ *flat, smooth, floating* .... 183 **Aquática.**
(Aquatic.)

London, Publifhed by D. Thornton, 1812.

j

Clafs III. TRIANDRIA, continued.

DISCRIMINATING CHARACTERS.

Species

13 Elymus (Lyme-Grafs) .... **Elymus**

drooping; Spiculæ 4-flowered; Calyx-glumes setaceous; Leaves mucronate .... 184 Nutáns.
(Pendulous Sea)

erect { (Leaves erect, mucronate; Spiculæ 2 flowered, in a double series .... 185 Arenária.
(Upright Sea)

—— spreading, acuminate; ——— —— ——, triple ——— 186 Sylvática.
(Wood)

14 Melica (Melick-Grafs) .... **Mélica**

ros { pendulous; Panicle compact, 1 rowed .... 187 Nutáns.
(Nodding)

erect { —— few-flowered, branched .... 188 Uniflóra.
(1 flowered)

—— many —— , compact, purple; Root bulbous .... 189 Purpúrea.
(Purple)

15 Briza (Quaking-Grafs) .... **Briza**

ulæ { triangular; Stipulæ very long, lanceolate; Calyx longer than the floscules .... 190 Minor.
(Lefs)

ovate ; —— —— short, obtuse ; —— shorter —— ——— 191 Média.
(Middle)

16 Poa (Meadow-Grafs) .... **Poa**

Branches semiverticillate; Branchlets alternate; Floscules 5 to 8 ; Culm near 6 feet .... 192 Aquática.
(Aquatic)

—— —— ; —— binate ; —— 5; Culm 1 foot; Plant sea-green .... 193 Glaúca.
(Sea Green)

—— alternately branched; —— ; —— 4 ; —— short; —— above partiularly sea-green } .... 194 Alpína.
(Alpine)

—— —— decomposed, flowering horizontally patent; Floscules 5; Culm ¾ foot; Plant rough; Stipule long lanceolate acute .... 195 Setácea.
(Rough)

—— —— , —— ; —— 4 or 5; Culm 1 or ¾f.; Plant smooth; Stipule short obtuse. .... 196 Láeva.
(Smooth)

—— alternate, patent; Spikelets adprefsed to the branchlets; Floscules 8 to 12; Culm 1 foot .... 197 Flúitans.
(Flote)

—— semiverticillate, spicate or ramous, reflexed as if broken; —— 4 to 7; Culm near 1 foot .... 198 Retrofrácta.
(Reflexed)

—— binate, divaricate, nearly on one side; Floscules 3 to 9; Culm ½ foot, oblique, comprefsed .... 199 Annua.
(Annual)

—— semiverticillate ; —— 2 to 4; —— , erect, subcomprefsed .... 200 Nemorália.
(Wood)

—— subcondensate; Branchlets binate, flexuose; —— 3 ; —— afcending .... 201 Flexuósa.
(Zigzag)

—— ovate, subflexuose; Floscules 4; Culm 1 foot, erect, bulbous, subglaucous .... 202 Bulbósa.
(Bulbous)

Branchlets subflexuose; Floscules 3 to 9; —— —— very much comprefsed .... 203 Comprefsa.
(Comprefsed)

rigid, in a double order; —— 4 to 8; —— short, rigid, round, very smooth .... 204 Rigida.
(Stiff)

rather compact; Panicle erect; Branches often binate; Floscules 5; Root creeping, height a few inches .... 205 Maritima.
(Creeping Sea)

Rachis & Peduncles flexuose; Floscules 3 to 5; Stipulæ formed of cilæ; Culm 1 foot, decumbent .... 206 Decúmbens.
(Decumbent)

Floscules 4 to 5; Stipulæ rather acute, eroded; Culm 1 foot, proftrate .... 207 Procúmbens.
(Proftrate)

London, Publifhed by Dr. Thornton. 1812.

Tab. II *

Clafs III. TRIANDRIA, continued.

DISCRIMINATING CHARACTERS.

	Spécies
n. 47. Brómus *(Brome-Grafs)*	**Brómus**

Sect. I. Floscules 2-stamen'd

Panicle, erect, spreading .... 208 **Diándrus.**
(2-stamen'd)

Sect. II. Floscules 3-stamen'd.

spreading; Peduncles simple; Spikelets ovate, comprefsed, 9 to 12, flowered; Glumes smooth; 209 **Secalìnus.**
Culm 3 feet *(Smooth rye)*

———; ————— ; ———ovate-lanceolate, 12 to 16, ———; ——— downy; 210 **Lanuginósus.**
Culm 3 feet *(Downy rye)*

———; ————— ; ———roundifh-lanceolate 5 to 9, ——— scaled; 3 feet ...... 211 **Arvénsis.**
(Field)

diffuse; ————— ——— ; ———ovate; 7 flowered; Stem smooth .... 212 **Racemósus.**
(Racemed)

erect; Branches erect ; ———roundifh-lanceolate; 5 to 9 ; Stem erect; 3 feet ...... 213 **Eréctus.**
(Erect)

compact; Peduncles branched; ———ovate; 5 to 10, floscules, scaled, villous .... 214 **Móllis.**
(Soft)

Peduncles simple; Spikelets ovate, large; 12 to 16, floscules, scaled, smooth .... 215 **Multiflórus.**
(Many-flowered)

——— ——— ; ——— lanceolate; 6 to 8, scaled; Culm very leafy, ½ a foot ...... 216 **Stérilis.**
(Sterile)

——— branched; ——— ——— roundifh; 9, ———; 4 or 5 feet; Leaves rough ...... 217 **Asper.**
(Rough)

erect, simple, 2-rowed; Crowns shorter than the Glume; Leaves naked .... 218 **Pinnátus.**
(Pinnated)

nodding, ——— 1-rowed; ——— longer ——— — ———; ——— hairy .... 219 **Sylváticus.**
(Wood)

n. 48. Avéna *(Oat-Grafs)*	**Avéna**

erect, Calyx-glumes about 5 flowered; Leaves downy, height 1¼ foot .... 220 **Anguftifólius.**
(Narrow-leaved)

very much branched; nodding; Crown twisted; Culm 3 feet; Leaves rough; bristles brown .... 221 **Fátua.**
Calyx about 3-flowered. *(Wild or Mad)*

——— not ———; ——— 1¼ foot; ——— pubefcent; Panicle gold-coloured ...... 222 **Flavéscens.**
(Yellow)

subspicate, little branched; erect; Calyx about 3-flowered. Culm 1 to 2 feet; Leaves pubefcent .... 223 **Pubéscens.**
(Downy)

n. 49. Arúndo *(Reed)*	**Arúndo**

Calyx covered Panicle spreading; Floscules crownlefs; Culm 6 feet .... 224 **Phragmítes.**
(Common)

equal with the Corolla; Panicle erect, clustered; Flowers crownlefs; Culm 2 to 5 feet ...... 225 **Coloráta.**
(Coloured)

covered ———, patent; ——— imbricated, crowded; Culm 6 feet ...... 226 **Epigéios.**
(Lond)

longer than ——— , diffuse; ——— scattered, erect; Culm 3 to 4 ...... 227 **Calamagrostis.**
(Grafs-like)

——— , spiked; — — — erect, crownlefs; ——— 3 feet .... 228 **Arenária.**
(Lea)

London, Publifhed by D.ʳThornton, 1812.

Tab 12*

Clafs III. TRIANDRIA, continued.

DISCRIMINATING CHARACTERS.

Species

n.50.Festúca. *(Fescue-Grafs.)* .... Festúca

    compact;Floscules roundifh, smooth at the base; Culm square, a span high................229 Ovina.
    (Sheep.)

    ————; ———— compressed-keeled, pubescent; ——— ———, —— ——. ....230 Vivipera.
    (Viviparous.)

    diffuse; ———— crowned; ———— round, 1 to 2 feet...........................231 Duriúscula.
    (Hard.)

    ————; ———— round, indiftinctly nerved; ———— , 2 feet.....................232 Praténsis.
    (Meadow.)

    branched; ———— oblong, angular, crownlefs; ——— purple, 3 ....233 Calamária.
    (Reed-like.)

    ramous; ———— round, crowned;Root creeping; ——— decumbent, 1foot...........234 Rúbra.
    (Red.)

    subramous; Floscules awl-shaped, crowned, rough at the apex; Culm 6 to 12 Inches...........235 Bromoídes.
    (Brome-like.)

    nearly simple; ——— —— ————, ————1 Calyx very short; Culm angular a span.........236 Uniglúmis.
    (1-glumed.)

    nodding; ———— ————, ————rough at the apex; ——— 12 to 14 inches..............237 Murális.
    (Wall.)

    ————; ———— lanceolate, ventricose, crowned; Culm 3 to 4 feet................238 Gigantéa.
    (Giant.)

    ————; ———— round, indiftinctly nerved; ——— —— ———..................239 Elátior.
    (Tall.)

    elongated; Florets round, nervelefs, crownlefs; Culm erect, 2 feet....................240 Spicáta.
    (Spiked.)

n.51.Lólium. *(Darnel.)* .... Lóliun

    Crowned; Crown twice as long as the floscules; Spikelets shorter than the Calyx; Culm above 241 Aristátum.
    very rough, 2 feet *(Bearded.)*

    scarcely Crowned; Crown very small; Spikelets length of the Calyx; Culm very smooth, 1foot.242 Arvénse.
    (Field.)

    Crownlefs; ———————— longer than —— ; —— ———— .243 Perénne.
    (Perennial.)

n.52.Rottbóllia. *(Hard-Grafs.)* .... Rottbóllia

    Spike cylindrical, awl-shaped; bowed...244 Incurváta.
    (Incurved Sea.)

n.53.Hórdeum .... Hórdeum

    with long Crowns, intermediate, Calyx-glumes lanceolate, ciliate; Culm near a foot.........245 Murínum.
    (Wall.)

    lefser ———— Calyx-glumes all setaceous, rough; Culm ½ foot, decumbent at the base.........246 Praténse.
    (Meadow.)

    inner Calyx-glumes of the lateral florets semi-ovate; Culm ½ foot...................247 Marítimum.
    (Sea.)

n.54.Cynosúrus. *(Dogs-tail-Grafs.)* .... Cynosúrus

    simple, linear, bracteæ pectinated, crownlefs...................................248 Cristátus.
    (Crested.)

    compound, ovate; ———— pinnated, crowned................................249 Echinátus.
    (Echinated.)

n.55.Tríticum. *(Wheat-Grafs.)* .... Tríticum

    truncated, 6flowered; Culm purpleifh at the base; Leaves glaucous, 2 feet high..........250 Júnceum.
    (Rush.)

    subulate, ————; ——— erect, 2 feet; Root creeping........................251 Repens
    (Creeping)

    acuminate, 4————; ——— —— ——; Crowns longer than the valves of the Corolla....252 Aristátum.
    (Bearded.)

    obtuse, many————; ——— —— 3 inches; Crownlefs........................253 Marítimum.
    (Sea.)

London, Publifhed by Dr. Thornton. 1812.

Tab. 13.*

Class III. TRIANDRIA, continued.

DISCRIMINATING CHARACTERS.

Order III. Trigynia.

Species.

n. 56. Móntia. (Chickweed.) .... Móntia.

Stem much branched; Leaves opposite, spatulate .... 254 Fontána.
(Water.)

n. 57. Holósteum. (Chickweed.) .... Holósteum

Stem erect; Flowers white, in umbels .... 255 Umbelliferum.
(Umbelliferous.)

n. 58. Polycárpon. (All-seed.) .... Polycárpon

Stem much branched; Leaves 4 together; Flowers white, panicled .... 256 Tetraphýllum.
(4-leaved.)

Order IV. Monœcia.

n. 59. Bryónia. (Bryony.) .... Bryónia

Stem slender, voluble; Leaves palmate .... 257 Álba.
(White.)

n. 60. Amaránthus. (Amaranth.) .... Amaránthus

Stem diffuse; Leaves ovate .... 258 Blitum.
(Wild.)

n. 61. Spargánium. (Bur-reed.) .... Spargánium

branched, Leaves 3-sided, sides concave; Stem erect. 3 feet .... 259 Ramósum.
(Branched.)

udes { simple { ——— ———, —— flat; Stigma linear; Stem smaller ... 260 Símplex
(Simple.)

——— ———, —— ———; —— ovate; —— floating ... 261 Natans.
(Floating.)

n. 62. Týpha. (Reed-mace.) .... Týpha

somewhat ensiform; male & female ament approximate; Culm 6 feet ... 262 Latifólia.
(Broad-leaved.)

aves { semi-cylindrical; ——— —— —— remote; Culm 3 feet. .. 263 Angustifólia
(Narrow-leaved.)

linear; Culm 1 foot .... 264 Minor.
(Less.)

London, Published by Dr. Thornton, 1812.

Clafs III. TRIANDRIA, continued.

DISCRIMINATING CHARACTERS.

63 Cárex. *(Sedge.)* .... Cárex

Sect. I. Spike single, simple, 2 Stigmas.

{monœcious; Capsules reflexed, acuminate at both ends resembling fleas; Culm filiform 1f.ᵗ 265 Pulicáris.
(Flea.)

diœcious. {———, ovate, afcending, serrulated at the margin; Culm fcarce a span high smooth..266 Dióica.
! Diœcious

{——— lanceolate-triangular deflexed-spreading, angles scabrous at the apex.}.. 267 Davalliána.
Culm. about a span. smooth} *(Davall's.)*

Sect. II. Spike single, simple, 3 Stigmas.

was monœcious; Capsule spreading. subulate; Culm 3 to 5 inches................. 268 Pauciflóra
(Few-flowered.)

Sect. III Spikes several, monœcious, males above.

kelets dispersed { capitate; aril entire; Culm about 4 inches................. 269 Incúrva.
(Curved.)

spiked; ——— 2-cleft { male & female flowers intermixed; Culm 1f.ᵗ erect-incurved..270 Arenária
(Sea.)

{——— ——— ——— separate; ——— erect . 271 Intermédia.
(Intermediate.)

: somewhat { Root very creeping; Bractea leafy, erect; Fruit appressed................. 272 Dióica.
y compound. *(Divided.)*

fibrous { oblong, squarrose; Fruit divaricated, acuminate, cleft................. 273 Muricáta.
(Prickly.)

{ elongated, often branching at the base; Fruit nearly erect................. 274 Canescens⁺
(Grey.)

k twice or { spreading, paniculate-branched, acute; Culm 3-sided flat, 2 or 3 f.ᵗ................. 275 Paniculáta.
k compound. *(Great Panicled.)*

compact { acutish; Culm below 3-sided, prominent, above round, 1f.ᵗ................. 276 Teretiúscula.
(Roundish.)

{ obtuse; ——— 3-sided, sides excavated, 2 f.ᵗ................. 277 Excaváta.*
(Hollowed.)

Sect. IV Spikes several, monœcious, females above.

{ single. remote. almost sefsile; Culm 1 f.ᵗ................. 278 Remóta.
(Remote.)

about 3 together. { Fruit bifid at the mouth; Culm 1 to 3 f.ᵗ 279 Axilláris.
(Axilbary.)

{ ——— entire ——— ———; ——— 6 to 12 inches................. 280 Stelluláta.
(Prickly.)

6 of them { approximate; of a silvery-white; Culm triangular, angles rather rough, 1f.ᵗ 281 Álba.**
(White.)

{ rather remote; of a greenish-brown; --- ———, ——— smooth................. 282 Ovális.
(Oval-spiked.)

⁺Divúlsa. * Vulpína. **Cúrta.

London. Publifhed by D.ʳ Thornton, 1812.

Tab. 15*

Clafs III. TRIANDRIA, continued.

DISCRIMINATING CHARACTERS.

Sect. V. Spikes possessing distinct sexes: only 1 male; Bracteas membranous.

uses { channelled; Culm cespitose, 1 or 2 inches high .... 283 Clandestina.
(Secret.)

{ flat; Culm ascending, a span high .... 284 Digitáta.
(Digitate.)

Sect. VI. Spikes as in the last Sect. Bracteas leafy.

a Diandrous, Sheaths hardly any; Glumes ovate, black; Culm 1 f.t high or more .... 285 Atráta.
(Black.)

Digyneous : Sheath.

{ Glumes a feruginous-brown; Fruit elliptic, inflated, somewhat beaked, emarginate; Culm a span .... 286 Pulla.
(Rufset.)

—— a deep black; Fruit compressed, thickly imbricated; Culm a span Leaves rigid 287 Rigida.
(Rigid.)

—— of the male-flower brown; Fruit permanent; Culm a span .... 288 Cæspitósa.
(Tufted.)

—— —— —— black; —— deciduous; —— 1 to 2 f.t Leaves stiff & strait 289 Stricta.
(Strait-leaved.)

none } Female spikes sessile, clustered, roundish; Fruit roundish, villous; Culm generally recumbent a span. .... 290 Pilulifera.
(Round-headed.)

ree any } —— —— pendulous, greenish; Fruit spreading, furrowed, beaked; Culm 1 f.t or more. Male spike erect; glumes ovate; Crowns long, rough. 291 Bseudocypérus.
(Bastard Cyperus.)

Short

{ Fruit beaked, bowed-deflexed; Glumes tawny, nerve green, margin white; Culm a span .... 292 Flava.
(Yellow.)

—— roundish pubescent; —— feruginous; Anthers sulphur-coloured; —— —— 293 Præcox.
(Vernal.)

—— elliptical 3-sided, roughish; Glume brown, or blackish; Culm a foot .... 294 Recúrva.
(Recurved.)

y short

{ —— —— inflated obtuse; Spikes cylindrical peduncled when fruit bearing pendulous; Culm 1 to 1½ f.t 295 Palléscens.
(Pale.)

—— ovate; Female spikes roundish, bracteas very long; Culm a span. 296 Exténsa.
(Long Bracteated.)

—— tomentous; —— —— nearly sessile; Culm 1 f.t 297 Tomentósa.
(Downy-fruited.)

u short bundles

{ Fruit ovate, triangular, beaked; Spike filiform, rather loose, nodding; Culm 2 to 3 f.t 298 Sylvática.
(Wood.)

{ acuminate; Spike filiform, rather loose, nodding; Culm an hand. 299 Capilláris.
(Capillary.)

—— Fruit inflated, beaked; Female spike erect, few-flowered; Culm 1½ f.t 300 Depauperáta.
(Starved.)

gated

{ nearly equal to the peduncle; Spikes cylindrical, very long, nodding; Fruit greatly crowded, ovate, acute. 301 Péndula.
(Great Pendulous.)

—— —— ; —— filiform, lax, a little nodding; Fruit lanceolate, triangular, nerved. 302 Strigósa.
(Strigose.)

—— —— ; —— oblong, very remote .... 303 Dístans.
(Loose.)

shorter than the —— ; —— ovate; Fruit beaked straight .... 304 Fúlva.
(Tawny.)

—— —— ; —— cylindrical, remote, often compound; Fruit 2 nerved 305 Binérvis.
(2-nerved.)

half the length of the —— ; —— rather loose, —— ; Fruit inflated .... 306 Panícea.
(Pink leaved.)

London, Published by Dr. Thornton, 1812.

Tab. 16*

Class III. TRIANDRIA, concluded.

DISCRIMINATING CHARACTERS.

Sect. VII Spikes possessing distinct sexes, males numerous.

Cárex
concluded.

males 2, & not 3; Spikes filiform... 307 Acúta.
teeth:
(Acute.)

long; Spikes cylindrical, females peduncled...................... 308 Lœvigáta.
(Smooth-stalked.)

rly equal to the peduncles. { Fruit hairy................................ 309 Hírta.
(Hairy.)

___ villous........................... 310 Filifórmis.
(Slender-leaved.)

rarely sheathed. { Spikes cylindrical, rather obtuse, erect, female with crown-pointed glumes, 311 Paludósa.
male with obtuse. (Marsh.)

Glumes all obtuse................................... 312 Micheliána.
(Michelis.)

short; Spikes erect, female cylindrical; Glumes all acuminate; Fruit beaked, bifurcate... 313 Ripária
(Bank.)

Fruit ovate.. 314 Vesicária.
(Bladder.)

___ globular.. 316 Ampullácea.
(Pitcher.)

Order V Diæcia.

64 Empétrum. (Crakeberry.)... **Empétrum**
316 Nigrum.
(Black.)

Order VI Polygamia.

65 Hólcus. (Soft-Grass.).. **Hólcus**

villous; Bisexual flower inferior. Male with a bowed-recurved crown Culms several 317 Lanátus.
erect, 1½ ft high. (Woolly.)

almost naked; ___ ___ ___, ___ ___ geniculate crown (not bowed); Culm 318 Móllis.
single, procumbent. (Soft.)

smooth; ___ ___ superior. ___ ___ refracted crown; Culm 3 or 4 ft 319 Avenáceus.
(Oat-like.)

66 Egílops. (Hard-Grass.).. **Egílops**

Spike very slender, curved; Culm 6 inches high.................... 320 Incurváta.
(Curved.)

London, Published by Dr Thornton, 1812.

Clafs IV. TETRANDRIA. Four Stamina.

DISCRIMINATING CHARACTERS.

Order 1 Monogynia.

Species.

n.67 Scabióſa. (Scabious.) .... Scabióſa

4-cleft { equal; Leaves entire; Root premorse .... 321 Succiſa.
(Devil's-bib.)

radiating; —— incised, pinnatifid; Root fusiform .... 322 Arvénsis.
(Field.)

5-cleft, radiate .... 323 Minor.
(Small.)

n.68 Dípsacus (Teasel.) .... Dípsacus.

ovate { Involucre reflexed; Chaffs recurved; Stem 5 feet ... 324 Fullónum.
(Fullers.)

—— inflexed; —— straight; —— leſs tall .... 325 Sylvéstris.
(Wild.)

roundiſh, about the size of a nutmeg; Involucre deflexed; Leaves petioled, appendaged; 326 Pilóſus.
Stem from 2 to 3 f.ᵗ Chaffs, pubescent, with ciliated setæ. (Hairy.)

n.69 Rúbia (Madder.) .... Rúbia

Leaves in fours .... 327 Sylvéstris.
(Wild.)

n.70 Gálium (Bed-straw.) .... Gálium

ovate; Stem simple above, hairy; Fruit smooth .... 328 Cruciátum.
(Croſs-wort.)

obovate; —— diffuse, branched above; —— —— .... 329 Palústre.
(Water.)

lanceolate; —— erect; Fruit hispid .... 330 Boreále.
(Northern.)

lanceolate, crowned, ciliate .... 331 Witheríngii.
(Witherings.)

obovate, obtuse, mucronate; Stem proſtrate .... 332 Saxátile.
(Rock.)

lanceolate, crowned at the apex; Stem weak .... 333 Uliginóſum.
(Marsh.)

lanceolate, mucronate; Stem curved .... 334 Muríne.
(Wall.)

lanceolate; Fruit hispid .... 335 Aparíne.
(Goose Graſs.)

—— aculeate-serrulated forward; Fruit smooth .... 336 Eréctum.
(Erect.)

—— margin & stem aculeate backward .... 337 Tricórne.
(3-horned.)

linear-lanceolate, mucronate, very entire .... 338 Puſíllum.
(Least.)

linear, furrowed; Flowers panicled & heaped .... 339 Vérum.
(True.)

elliptical; Flowers panicled, divaricate; Stem 2 to 4 feet .. 340 Mollúgo.
(Great Hedge.)

London, Publiſhed by Dᴿ Thornton, 1812.

Tab. 18*

Clafs IV. TETRANDRIA, continued.

DISCRIMINATING CHARACTERS.

Species.

n. 1 Aspérula (Woodruff.) .... **Aspérula**

{ 4 together, linear; Fruit smooth .... 341 Odoráta.
(Odorous.)

{ ———, lanceolate; ——— hispid .... 342 Cynánchica.
(Throat-wort.)

n. 2 Sherárdia (Sherardia.) .... **Sherárdia**

Leaves all verticillate .... 343 Arvénsis.
(Wild.)

n. 3 Exacum (Gentianella.) .... **Éxacum**

Leaves sessile; Stem filiform, dichotomous .... 344 Filiforme.
(Filiform.)

n. 4 Plantágo (Plantain.) .... **Plantágo**

ovate { shorter than the petiole, smoothish; Seeds numerous .... 345 Major.
(Greater.)

{ longer ——— ——— ———, pubescent; ——— single ... 346 Incána.
(Hoary.)

ves lanceolate, acute at each end; Scape angular, in the others cylindrical .... 347 Lanceoláta.
(Lanceolate.)

linear { mostly entire 348

{ pinnated, dentate, deprefsed like a star; Anthers terminated by a lanceolate membrane. 349 Corónopus.
(Buck's-horn.)

n. 5 Centúnculus (Pimpernel.) .... **Centúnculus**

Leaves roundish, alternate; Stems procumbent, 4 or 5 inches .... 350 Minimus.
(Little.)

n. 6 Sanguisórba (Burnet.) .... **Sanguisórba**

Leaves pinnated; Stem 3 feet .... 351 Officinális.
(Officinal.)

n. 7 Epimédium (Barren-wort.) .... **Epimédium**

Leaves more than decompound .... 352 Alpínum
(Alpine.)

n. 8 Córnus (Cornel-tree.) .... **Córnus**

{ arboreous; Branches straight, blood-coloured .... 353 Sanguínea
(Red.)

{ herbaceous; Stems a span high .... 354 Mínima.
(Dwarf.)

n. 9 Alchemilla (Ladies-Mantle.) .... **Alchémilla**

{ 7 to 9-lobed, crenate-serrated, plaited .... 355 Vulgáris.
(Common.)

{ 5-lobed, serrated, silky beneath .... 356 Alpína.
(Alpine.)

{ 3-lobed, crenate-incised, flat .... 357 A———
(———)

London, Publijhed by Dr Thornton, 1812.

Claſs IV. TETRANDRIA, continued.

DISCRIMINATING CHARACTERS.

Order II Digynia.   *Species*

280 Buffónia. *(Buffonia)* .... Buffónia

   Leaves subulate, connate .... 358 Tennifólia.
                   (Slender-leaved.)

Order III Tetragynia

281 Ílex *(Holly.)* .... Ílex

   Leaves ovate, acute, spinous .... 359 Aquifólium.
                   (Holly-Tree.)

282 Tillǽa *(Tillæa)* .... Tillǽa

   Stems procumbent, flowers sessile, mostly 3-cleft .... 360 Muſcósa.
                   (Mossy.)

283 Potamogéton *(Pond-weed.)* .... Potamogéton
   Herb.   *Leaves.*
   floating; *oblong-ovate, petioled* .... 361 Nátans.
                   (Floating.)
   immersed; *ovate, opposite, very spreading crowded; Spike 4-flowered* ...... 362 Dénſum.
                   (Close-leaved.)
   ————; *ovate-lanceolate, attenuated into petioles, a bright green; Spike many-flowered.* 363 Lúcens.
                   (Shining.)
   ————; *lanceolate, alternate, undulated, serrated* .... 364 Críspum.
                   (Curled.)
   ————; ————, *opposite, acuminate, setaceous* .... 365 Setáceum.
                   (Setaceous.)
   ————; *cordate, embracing the stem* .... 366 Perfoliátum.
                   (Perfoliate.)
   ————; *linear, most narrow, patent at the base; Stem round* .... 367 Pusíllum.
                   (Small.)
   ————; ————; *Stem compreſsed* .... 368 Compréſsum.
                   (Flat-stalked.)
   ————; *linear-lanceolate, alternate, Stem somewhat dichotomous, crowded with leaves* .... 369 Gramíneum.
                   (Grass-leaved.)
   ————; *2-rowed, approximate, near 2 inches long* .... 370 Pectinátum.
                   (Pectinated.)

284 Radíola *(Radiola).* .... Radíola

   Leaves sessile, ovate; Stem dichotomous, 1 or 2 inches high ...... 371 Millegrána.
                   (All-Seed.)

285 Sagína *(Pearl-wort.)* .... Sagína

   procumbent; Petals very short; Stem smooth .... 372 Procúmbens.
                   (Procumbent)
Stem { *almost upright; —— indistinct; —— pubescent* .... 373 Ápetala.
                   (Apetalled.)
   erect; —— conspicuous, entire; Stem smooth .... 374 Erécta.
                   (Upright)

286 Rúppia *(Ruppia.)* .... Rúppia

   Leaves setaceous, immersed .... 375 Marítima.
                   (Sea.)

London, Publiſhed by D.ʳ Thornton, 1811.

Tab. 20.*

Clafs IV. TETRANDRIA, continued.

DISCRIMINATING CHARACTERS.

Order IV. Monœcia.

Species

a.87. Betulá. (Birch.) .... **Betulá**

kom { a Shrub, 3 f.^t high; Leaves roundifh, crenate, reticulate-veined beneath .... 376 **Naua.** (Dwarf.)

a Tree { lofty, bark snowny-white, epiderm paper like; Branches erect; Leaves ovate .... 377 **Alba.** (White.)

not large nor erect; Branches tortuous, spreading; Leaves roundifh, wedge-shaped repand, serrated, glutinous, veins underneath, villous at the axil. } 378 **Alnus.** (Common Alder.)

a.88. Búxus. (Box.) .... **Búxus**

A low evergreen shrub; Flowers axillary, clustered, yellowifh; Anthers ovate-sagittate .... 379 **Sempervívum** (Evergreen.)

a.89. Eriocáulon. (Pipewort.) .... **Eriocáulon**

Stem 7-angled; Leaves acuminate, formed of reticulated cells ...... 380 **Septanguláre.** (Seven-Angled)

a.90. Littoréla. (Shoreweed.) .... **Littoréla**

Herb stemlefs; Leaves linear, very entire .... 381 **Lacustris.** (Marsh)

Gen.91. Urtica. (Nettle.) .... **Urtica**

monœcious { female capitate; males panicled; Leaves ovate; Stem 2 f.^t .... 382 **Pilulifera.** (Headed)

in simple racemes; Leaves elliptical; Stem 1 f.^t .... 383 **Minor.** (Lefs)

diœcious, sometimes monœcious, in racemes much branched, 2 together, Leaves cordate; Stem 3 f.^t 384 **Dióica.** (Diœcious)

Order V. Diœcia

a.92. Myrica. (Sweet-Gale.) .... **Myrica**

Stem shrubby, 3 f.^t much branched; Leaves lanceolate, slightly serrated ...... 385 **Odoráta.** (Odorous)

a.93. Hippopháe. (Buckthorn) .... **Hippopháe**

A Shrub, 8 f.^t branches spread, straight, stiff, sharp; Leaves lanceolate .... 386 **Maritima.** (Sea)

a.94. Viscum. (Mifsletoe.) .... **Viscum**

Stem dichotomous; Leaves lanceolate .... 387 **Album.** (White)

Order VI. Polygámia.

a.95. Valántia. (Valantia.) .... **Valántia**

Leaves 4 together, elliptic-oblong, 3-nerved, reticulated .... 388 **Cruciáta.** (Grofs-wort)

a.96. Parietária. (Pellitory of the Wall.) .... **Parietária**

Stem reddifh, jointed, 1½ high; Leaves lanceolate, ovate .... 389 **Officinális** (Officinal)

London, Publifhed by Dr Thornton. 1812.

Tab. 21*

Clafs IV. TETRANDRIA, continued.

DISCRIMINATING CHARACTERS.

Order VII. Didynamia.   Species

97. Leonúrus. (Motherwort.)...Leonúrus

    Leaves upper, lanceolate, 3-lobed or entire...................390 Cardíaca.
                                                (Cordial.)

98. Glecóma. (Ground-Ivy.)..Glecóma

    Leaves reniform, crenate..391 Hederácea.
                                                (Common.)

99. Melíttis. (Melittis.)..Melittis

    { 3-lobed ....392 Melifsophýllum
                                    (Balm-leaved.)
  ar{ 1-lobed ....393 Grandiflóra.
                                    (Large-flowering.)

100. Prunélla. (Self-Peal.)...Prunélla

    Leaves ovate-oblong, petioled......................................394 Vulgáris.
                                           (Common.)

101. Stáchys. (Wound-wort.)..Stáchys

    { many-flowered; Leaves, crenate; Stem woolly...............395 Lanáta.
                                          (Downy.)
  ails{   { __ sefsile, half amplexicaul, linear-lanceolate .....396 Palústris.
                                          (Marsh.)
    { 6-flowered ....{   (inferior lip variegated with white & purple.....397 Sylvática.
                                             (Hedge.)
            { petioled{ __ a light purple ....398 Arvénsis.
                                        (Field.)

102. Méntha. (Mint.)..Méntha

      Sect. 1. Flowers Spiked or Capitate.

    { (Leaves elliptical, obtuse, wrinkled, crenate, villous beneath.....399 Rotundifólia.
    { Spikes interrupted{   (Round-leaved.)
 es{   { __ lanceolate, acute, naked...................400 Viridis.
 ile   (Green.)
    { __ hardly interrupted; Leaves dentate-serrated, chiefly tomentous beneath.....401 Sylvéstris.
                                             (Wild.)

    { (very smooth at the base; Leaves somewhat ovate, smoothish.....402 Piperíta.
    { Calyx smooth....{   (Pepper.)
 __{   { __ every where; __ cordate, naked on both sides.....403 Odoráta.
 lal   (Odorous.)
    { __ hirsute; Leaves ovate...........................404 Hirsúta.
                                            (Hairy.)

      Sect. II. Flowers verticillate.

 ile{ Pedicels altogether smooth; Leaves lanceolate...............405 Grácilis.
                                           (Slender-leaved.)

    { Calyx & Pedicels smooth; Leaves ovate; Stem flexuose.....406 Rubra.
    {   (Red.)
    { __ __ __ at the base; Leaves ovate; Stem much branched.....407 Ramósa.
    {   (Bushy.)
 led{ __ __ hirsute; Leaves ovate-lanceolate, acute on both sides.....408 Acutifólia.
    {   (Sharp-leaved.)
    { __ __ : __ elliptic-ovate; Calyx bell-shaped.....409 Arvénsis.
    {   (Field.)
    { __ tomentose; __ ovate; Stem proftrate.....410 Pulégium.
                                          (Penny-royal.)

London. Published by D.r Thornton. 1812.

Tab. 22.*

Clafs IV. TETRANDRIA, continued.

DISCRIMINATING CHARACTERS.

Species

103. Scutellária. (Scull-cap.) .... Scutellária

Leaves { cordate-lanceolate, crenate, wrinkled; Stem 1 or 2 f. .... 411 Major. (Large.)

{ cordate-ovate, almost very entire; ———— a few inches. .... 412 Minor. (Lefs.)

104. Thymus. (Thyme.) .... Thymus

Flrs. { headed; Stem decumbent. .... 413 Serpillum. (Wild.)

{ verticill'd { 6-flowered, peduncled simple. .... 414 Acinós. (Basil.)

{ many-flowered, dichotomous. { Calyx hairs included. .... 415 Calamintha. (Common.)

{ ———— ———— projecting. .... 416 Nepeta. (Lefs.)

105. Origanum. .... Origanum

Spikes roundish, panicled conglomerate, smooth. .... 417 Vulgáre. (Marjoram.)

106. Clinopódium. .... Clinopódium

Verticils hispid. .... 418 Vulgáre. (Basil.)

107. Ballóta. (Horehound.) .... Ballóta

Leaves ovate, undivided, serrated. .... 419 Nigra. (Black.)

108. Marrúbium. (Horehound.) .... Marrúbium

Calyx-teeth, 10, setaceous, hooked. .... 420 Vulgáre. (White.)

109. Teucrium. (Germander.) .... Teucrium

Leaves { sefsile, oblong, dentate-serrate; Flowers in pairs. .... 421 Aquáticum. (Water.)

{ petioled { cordate, serrated ; ———— 1-rowed. .... 422 Nemorósum (Wood.)

{ ovate, incised-crenate; ———— ternate. .... 423 Murinum. (Wall.)

110. Ajuga. (Bugle.) .... Ajuga

Flrs. { solitary, axillary, subsefsile. .... 424 Chamæpitys (Ground Pine.)

{ several in verticils { having stolons; Leaves elliptic or obovate. .... 425 Reptans. (Creeping.)

{ without ———— { verticils crowded in a pyramidal form. .... 426 Pyramidális (Pyramidal.)

{ ———— rather remote. .... 427 Alpina. (Alpine.)

111. Betónica. (Betonica.) .... Betónica

Spike interrupted, middle segment of the lip emarginate. .... 428 Officinális. (Officinal.)

112. Galeópsis. (Hemp-nettle.) .... Galeópsis

Stem internodes { equal { helmit of the Corolla crenate-incised; Leaves villous. .... 429 Villósa. (Villous.)

{ ———— ———— indistinctly crenate; Leaves hairy. .... 430 Rubrum. (Red.)

{ thicker above { helmit ventricose. .... 431 Versicolor (Vary-coloured.)

{ ———— straightish. .... 432 Comm.

London, Publifhed by D! Thornton

Tab. 23.*

Clafs IV. TETRANDRIA, continued.

DISCRIMINATING CHARACTERS.

Species

x 113. Galeóbdolon. *(Dead-Nettle.)* .... **Galeóbdolon**

  Flowers yellow; Throat spotted with red .... 433 Lúteum.
                  (Yellow.)

114. Népeta. *(Cat-Mint.)* .... **Népeta**

  Corolla white, apex red, dotted .... 434 Catária.
                 (Cat-Mint.)

t 115. Lámium. *(Archangle.)* .... **Lámium**

  Leaves { petioled { cordate, acuminate; Flowers white; Anthers black .... 435 Album.
                  (White.)

         obtuse; ——— purple; ——— red .... 436 Purpúreum.
                  (Red.)

   upper sefsile, embracing the stem; Flowers beautifully rose-coloured .... 437 Amplexicaul.
                  (Amplexicaul.)

n 116. Orobánche. *(Broom-rape.)* .... **Orobánche**

  Stamina { naked, smooth; Corolla inflated; Style pubescent .... 438 Major.
                  (Greater.)

    clothed { pubescent; Segments of the lip acute; Style smooth .... 439 Elátior.
                  (Tall.)

      ciliate, middle segment lobed; —————— .... 440 Minor.
                  (Lefs.)

t 117. Euphrásia .... **Euphrásia**

  Leaves ovate, streaked, finely toothed .... 441 Officinális.
                  (Official.)

t 118. Rhinánthus. *(Yellow-Rattle.)* .... **Rhinánthus**

  Leaves lanceolate, serrated, upper lip of the Corolla arched .... 442 Cristæ Galli.
                  (Cock's-comb.)

t 119. Lathrǽa. *(Tooth-wort.)* .... **Lathrǽa**

  Root flefhy with cordate scales; Flowers pendulous .... 443 Squamária.
                  (Scaly.)

120. Bártsia. *(Bartsia.)* .... **Bártsia**

  Leaves { opposite, cordate-ovate; Anthers hirsute .... 444 Alpína.
                  (Alpine.)

    upper alternate { Flowers lateral; Anthers hirsute .... 445 Viscósa.
                  (Viscid.)

      1-rowed; ——— smooth .... 446 Rubra.
                  (Red.)

t 121. Melampýrum. *(Cow-wheat.)* .... **Melampýrum**

  Flowers { in conical spikes .... 447 Cristátum.
                  (Crested.)

    in quadrangular spikes .... 448 Arvénse.
                  (Corn-Field.)

    in pairs, lateral, 1-rowed { Corolla closed .... 449 Praténse.
                  (Meadow Field.)

      ——— open .... 450 Sylváticum.
                  (Wood.)

London, Publifhed by Dr. Thornton, 181_.

Tab. 34.*

Class IV. TETRANDRIA, concluded.

DISCRIMINATING CHARACTERS.

Species

n.122. Sibthórpia (Money-worth.) .... **Sibthórpia**

   Leaves kidney-shaped, somewhat peltate, crenate. .... 451 Peltáta.
   (Peltated.)

n.123. Linnéa (Linnéa.) .... **Linnéa**

   Branches 2-flowered; Corolla bell-shaped, nodding. .... 452 Boreális.
   (Northern.)

n.124. Limosélla. (Mudwort.) .... **Limosélla**

   Scape, shorter than the leaves, 1-flowered. .... 453 Aquática.
   (Aquatic.)

n.125. Digitális. (Foxglove.) .... **Digitális**

   Corolla bell-shaped, 5-cleft, curiously spotted with purple. ... 454 Purpúrea.
   (Purple.)

n.126. Scrophulária. (Figwort.) .... **Scrophulária**

Stem { winged: Leaf cordate, petioled decurrent .... 455 Aquática.
   (Aquatic.)

 naked { Stem naked; Root tuberous, granulated .... 456 Nodósa.
   (Knotty.)

   { Leaves beneath downy .... 457 Scorodóni
   (Balm-leaved.)

   pilous { ____ ____ pilous, Flower yellow .... 458 Lútea.
   (Yellow.)

n.127. Antirrhínum. (Snapdragon.) .... **Antirrhínum**

Sect. I. Corolla hardly spurred.

owers { densely spiked; Calyx small; height 3 feet .... 459 Majus.
   (Great.)

   { loosely ____ ; ____ longer than the Corolla, about 1 foot ... 460 Minus.
   (Least.)

Sect. II. Corolla with long spurs.

ons mbent { Leaves cordate, alternate; Stem striking roots .... 461 Cymbalária
   (Ivy-leaved.)

   ____ hastate. .... 462 Elatíne.
   (Sharp-pointed.)

   ____ ovate, ... 463 Ovátum.
   (Round-leaved.)

erect { ____ linear, glaucous, verticillate or scattered; Root creeping ... 464 Repens.
   (Creeping.)

   ____ lanceolate, mostly alternate, obtuse. .... 465 Minus.
   (Least.)

   ____ lanceolate-linear, crowded. .... 466 Lútea Vulgá
   (Common Yellow)

n.128. Pediculáris. (Louse-wort.) .... **Pediculáris**

Stem { single, branched .... 467 Palústris.
   (Marsh.)

   { many, simple, spreading .... 468 Praténsi
   (Pasture.)

London. Published by D. Thornton. 1812.

Tab. 25.*

Clafs V. PENTANDRIA, Five Stamina.

DISCRIMINATING CHARACTERS.

Order I. Monogynia.   Species

1.129. Echiúm. (Viper's-Buglofs.) .... Echiúm

nikes { erect-spreading, very hirsute .... 469 Album.
(White.)

deflexed, hairy .... 470 Vulgáre.
(Common Blue.)

1.130. Pulmonária. (Lung-wort.) .... Pulmonária

blas { nearly the length of the tube .... 471 Officinális.
(Officinal.)

short: Leaves glaucous .... 472 Marítima.
(Sea.)

1.131. Lithospérmum. (Gromwell.) .... Lithospérmum

olla { greatly exceeding the length of the Calyx; Leaves veinlefs .... 473 Purpúreum.
(Purple.)

scarcely _____ Calyx { Leaves veinlefs; Seeds rugose .... 474 Arvénse.
(Corn.)

_____ veined; _____ smooth .... 475 Officinále.
(Officinal.)

n.132. Anchúsa. (Alkanet.) .... Anchúsa

ives { ovate; Peduncles axillary, capitate .... 476 Sempervirens
(Evergreen.)

lanceolate; Spikes imbricated, 1-rowed .... 477 Officinális.
(Officinal.)

1.133. Asperúgo. (Madwort.) .... Asperúgo

Calyx of the fruit flattened; Stem procumbent .... 478 Procumbens.
(Procumbent.)

134. Cynoglófsum. (Hound's-tongue.) .... Cynoglófsum

res { broad-lanceolate, tomentous .... 479 Officinále.
(Officinal.)

spatulate-lanceolate, nakedifh .... 480 Sylvaticum.
(Wood.)

1.135. Lycópsis. (Buglofs.) .... Lycópsis

Leaves lanceolate, hispid; Calyx erect when flowering .... 481 Arvénsis.
(Corn.)

136. Myosótis. (Scorpion-Grafs.) .... Myosótis

Leaves elliptic-lanceolate; Spike curled .... 482 Scorpioides.
(Spiked.)

137. Borágo. (Borage.) .... Borágo

Leaves alternate; Calyx spreading .... 483 Officinále.
(Officinal.)

138. Sýmphytum. (Comfrey.) .... Sýmphytum

ives { ovate-lanceolate, decurrent .... 484 Officinále.
(Officinal.)

ovate semidecurrent .... 485 Tub
Tu..

Tab. 26.*

Clafs V. PENTANDRIA, continued.

DISCRIMINATING CHARACTERS.

Species

139. Anagállis. (Pimpernel.) .... Anagállis

{ ovate, dotted beneath; Stem procumbent .... 486 Arvénsis. (Corn.)

les { roundifh, no such marks; Stem creeping .... 487 Uliginósa. (Bog.)

140. Lysimáchia. (Loose-strife.) .... Lysimáchia

{ terminal; Leaves 3 or 4 at each joint .... 488 Vulgáris. (Common.)

les { lateral, in bunches; Leaves in pairs .... 489 Thyrsiflóra. (Tufted.)

141. Hottónia. (Water-violet.) .... Hottónia

Stem many-flowered; Peduncles verticillate .... 490 Palústris. (Marsh.)

142. Chirónia. (Centaury.) .... Chirónia

{ dichotomously panicled; Leaves ovate-lanceolate ...... 491 Commúnis. (Common.)

m { much branched on all sides; —— ovate .... 492 Ramósa. (Branched.)

143. Verbáscum. (Mullein.) .... Verbáscum

{ decurrent, tomentous on both sides .... 493 Magnum. (Great.)

{ embracing the stem, smooth .... 494 Blattária. (Moth.)

{ oblong-wedge-shaped, almost naked on the upper surface ... 495 Album. (White.)

s { oblong-cordate, sometimes pubescent, petioled, crenate, undulated ... 496 Nigrum. (Black.)

{ oblong-lanceolate, sessile, dentate .... 497 Virgátum. (Virgate.)

{ ovate-oblong, powdery on both sides .... 498 Pulveruléntum. (Powdered.)

144. Polemónium. (Greek Valerian.) .... Polemónium

Leaves pinnate: Flowers blue .... 499 Cœrúleum. (Blue.)

145. Cýclamen. (Sowbread.) .... Cýclamen

Corolla retroflexed .... 500 Vernum. (Spring.)

146. Solánum. (Night-shade.) .... Solánum

{ shrubby, climbing, berries red .... 501 Scandens. (Climbing.)

{ herbaceous, berries black .... 502 Nigrum. (Black.)

147. Vinca. (Periwinkle.) .... Vinca

{ rather upright; Leaves ovate, ciliate .... 503 Májor. (Greater.)

{ procumbent; —— elliptic-lanceolate, margin smooth ... 504 Mínor. (Lesser.)

London, Publifhed by Dr. Thornton, 1812.

Tab. 27.*

Class V. PENTANDRIA, continued.

DISCRIMINATING CHARACTERS.

Species

48. Azalea. *(Azalea.)* .... **Azálea**

Branches diffuse, procumbent .... 506 Procumbens.
(Trailing.)

49. Átropa. *(Nightshade.)* .... **Átropa**

Stem herbaceous; Leaves ovate, entire .... 506 Belladonna.
(Deadly.)

50. Convólvulus. *(Bindweed.)* .... **Convólvulus**

reniform .... 507 Maritima.
(Sea.)

sagittate { acute on both sides .... 508 Arvensis.
(Field.)

truncated behind .... 609 Sepium.
(Hedge.)

51. Menyánthes. *(Buckbean.)* .... **Menyánthes**

ternate: Corolla very villous on the upper surface ...... 510 Trifoliáta.
(3-leaved.)

cordate, waved; Corolla ciliated .... 511 Fimbriáta.
(Fringed.)

52. Prímula. *(Primrose.)* .... **Prímula**

crenate, smooth, powdered beneath .... 512 Farinósa.
(Powdered.)

dentated wrinkled { Scape 1-flowered; Limb of the Corolla flat ...... 513 Vulgáris.
(Common.)

many-flowered { Limb — — — — — ...... 514 Elátior.
(Oxlip.)

— — — — concave. ...... 515 Veris.
(Cowslip.)

53. Hyoscýamus. *(Henbane.)* .... **Hyoscýamus**

Leaves embrace the stem; Flowers sessile .... 516 Niger.
(Purple.)

54. Datúra. *(Thorn-apple.)* .... **Datúra**

Capsule erect, ovate, spinous .... 517 Stramónium.
(Stramonium.)

55. Campánula. *(Bell-flower.)* .... **Campánula**

reniform, the root-leaves, stem-leaves linear; Flowers somewhat panicled, blue ...... 518 Rotundifólia.
(Round-leaved.)

lanceolate-oval, stiff and straight; Panicle spreading ...... 519 Patulá.
(Spreading.)

— — — undulated; — — compact ...... 520 Rapúnculus.
(Rampion.)

lanceolate-linear, sessile, serrated; Stem leaves obovate; Flowers single, orbicular ...... 521 Persicifólia.
(Peach-leaved.)

ovate-lanceolate; Peduncles 1-flowered; Flowers large, blue-violet; Stem 3 or 4 feet ...... 522 Gigántea.
(Giant.)

cordate, 5-lobed; — — very long; — — blue ...... 523 Hederácea.
(Ivy-leaved.)

cordate-lanceolate; Flowers scattered 1-rowed, nodding; Root creeping ...... 524 Repens.
(Creeping.)

— — —; Peduncles axillary, few-flowered; Flowers violet ...... 525 Foliis Urtícæ.
(Nettle-leaved.)

ovate, crenate; Flowers terminal, & verticillate ...... 526 Glomeráta.
(Clustered.)

oblong, — — undulated; Flowers rotate-expanded, violet ...... 527 Hýbrida.
(Hybrid.)

London, Published by Dr Thornton, 1810.

Clafs V. PENTANDRIA, continued.

DISCRIMINATING CHARACTERS.

Species

56. Samolús. *(Brookweed.)* .... Samolús

Leaves obovate obtuse; Raceme many-flowered. .... 528 Aquáticus.
(Brookweed.)

57. Phyteúma. *(Rampion.)* .... Phyteúma

Leaves crenated, head roundish. .... 529 Orbiculáre.
(Round-headed.)

58. Lonicéra. *(Honeysuckle.)* .... Lonicéra

⎰peduncled, 2-flowered, ... 530 Erecta.
⎱ *(Upright.)*
rs ⎰ ⎰upper leaves perfoliate; Flowers verticillate .... 531 Perfoliáta.
⎱ ⎱ *(Perfoliate.)*
sefsile⎰all the leaves distinct; ——— in a head .... 532 Communis.
(Common.)

59. Rhámnus. *(Buckthorn.)* .... Rhámnus

⎰armed with terminal spines; Flowers generally dioicous ..... 533 Cathárticus.
es⎰ *(Cathartic.)*
⎱unarmed; Flowers bisexual .... 534 Frángula.
(Alder.)

60. Euonymús. *(Spindle-tree.)* .... Euonymús

Leaves lanceolate; Peduncles dichotomous .... 535 Commúnis.
(Common.)

61. Hederá. *(Ivy.)* .... Hederá

Leaves ovate & lobed .... 536 Commúnis.
(Common.)

62. Ríbes. *(Currants.)* .... Ríbes

Sect. I. Branches prickly.

⎰hirsute .... 537 Grofsulária.
rs⎰ *(Rough Gooseberry.)*
⎱smooth .... 538 Uva crispa.
(Smooth D?)

Sect. II. Branches unarmed.

⎰ ⎰hairy; Fruit black .... 539 Nigrum.
⎰pendulous⎰ *(Black.)*
⎰ ⎱smooth; ——— red .... 540 Rubrum.
nes⎰ *(Red.)*
⎰ ⎰Bracteæ longer than the flower .... 541 Alpínum.
⎱erect ⎰ *(Alpine.)*
⎱——— shorter —— ——— 542 Petroeum.
(Rock.)
Spike erect; Petals oblong. .... 543 Spicátum.
(Spiked.)

63. Gláux. *(Salt-wort.)* .... Gláux

Stem erect 3 inches high; Flowers single, axillary grows in Salt-marshes .... 544 Nigra.
(Black.)

64. Thésium. *(Toad flax.)* .... Thésium

Spike branched; Leaves linear-lanceolate .... 545 Linophýllum.
(Flax-leaved.)

65. Illecébrum. *(Knotgrass.)* .... Illecébrum

Flowers verticillate; Stems procumbent. .... 546 Verticillátum.
(Whorled.)

Tab. 29.*

Clafs V. PENTANDRIA, continued.

DISCRIMINATING CHARACTERS.

Order II. Diandria.

Species

166. Cuscúta. (Dodder.) — Cuscúta

- *ers* {
  - subsessile, without a crenated scale at the base of each stamen — 547 Major. (Greater.)
  - sessile: Stamina with minute crenated moon-shaped scales at the base — 548 Minor. (Lesser.)

167. Gentiána. (Gentian.) — Gentiána

- *olla* {
  - Bell-shaped, 5-cleft; Leaves linear — 549 Palustris. (Marsh.)
  - Funnel-shaped, ___; Stem many-flowered — 550 Nivális. (Alpine.)
  - Salver-shap'd {
    - 4-cleft; Throat beardless, outer calyx-segments larger — 551 Campéstris (Field.)
    - 5-cleft {
      - Segments crenate & appendaged at the base — 552 Vérna. (Spring.)
      - no such character, but with a throat bearded — 553 Autumnalis. (Autumnal.)

168. Swértia. (Swertia.) — Swértia

- Corolla 5-cleft, radical leaves ovate — 554 Palústris. (Marsh.)

169. Ulmús. (Elm.) — Ulmús

- *ers* {
  - subsessile, 4-cleft — 555 Campéstris. (Field.)
  - peduncled, 5 or 6-cleft — 556 Montána. (Mountain.)

170. Herniária. (Rupture-wort.) — Herniária

- *em & Leaves* {
  - smooth — 557 Glabra. (Smooth.)
  - hirsute — 558 Hirsúta. (Hairy.)

171. Sálsola. (Saltwort.) — Sálsola

- *eaves* {
  - spinous, subulate; Stem herbaceous decumbent — 559 Spinósa. (Prickly.)
  - unarmed, semicylindric; Stem shrubby, erect — 560 Fruticósa. (Shrubby.)

172. Chenopódium — Chenopódium

- *s* {
  - ovate {
    - very entire; Racemes cymous, divaricate, leafless — 561 Rotundifóliun (Round-leaved.)
    - dentate; ___ ___, much branched — 562 Latifólia. (Broad-leaved.)
  - subulate, semicylindrical; Flowers axillary, sessile — 563 Marítimum. (Sea.)
  - cordate, angular-dentate; Racemes subcymous, divaricate, leafless — 564 Hybrídum. (Hybrid.)
  - oblong, sinuate-repand, glaucous beneath; Racemes clustered, leafless — 565 Glaucum. (Glaucous.)
  - triangular, denticulated; Racemes crowded, very straight, almost leafless — 566 Erectum. (Erect.)
  - triangular-sagittate, very entire; Spikes compound, leafless — 567 Bonus Henricu (Good King Henry's.)
  - rhomboid-triangular, sinuate-dentate; Racemes erect, compound, leafy — 568 Rubrum. (Red.)
  - rhomboid-ovate, eroded, entire behind, powdery, upper ones oblong, entire; Seeds smooth — 569 Album. (White.)
  - ___ ___, very entire; Racemes conglomerate — 570 Olidium. (Stinking.)
  - hastate-sinuated; Seeds dotted — 571 Ficifólium. (Fig-leaved.)

173. Béta. (Beet.) — Béta

- Flowers in pairs; Stems decumbent — 572 Marítim

Breinigsville, PA USA
19 January 2010
231021BV00001B/24/A